YOUR CHILD WITH DEPRESSION

HOW TO KEEP THEM ALIVE

JEN TSANG

BALBOA.PRESS
A DIVISION OF HAY HOUSE

Balboa Press books may be ordered through booksellers or by contacting:

Balboa Press
A Division of Hay House
1663 Liberty Drive
Bloomington, IN 47403
www.balboapress.com
844-682-1282

Print information available on the last page.

ISBN: 979-8-7652-5681-7 (sc)
ISBN: 979-8-7652-5682-4 (hc)
ISBN: 979-8-7652-5680-0 (e)

Library of Congress Control Number: 2024923071

Balboa Press rev. date: 01/28/2025

To my daughter,

You are the bravest person I have ever known.

I love you more than anything.

Unwaveringly

to

Infinity.

CONTENTS

CONTENTS

INTRODUCTION

During the times that my child was crippled with severe depression I learned a lot. Some of the most important things that I have learned came directly from my child. She told me how it felt, what thoughts were in her head and how dark and hopeless it could be.

My child's insights were helpful to me in being able to understand the disorder and how best to care for her when she was suffering. More importantly, having this information helped me avoid making the situation worse. I believe that what my child taught me and my willingness to adapt my own behavior, helped keep her alive during the most difficult times.

My child explained severe depression to me in a way that I did not learn from mental health professionals. We talked about many difficult aspects of the condition that are often not discussed openly in society. She and I have made it to the other side of this experience and we would like to share some key "dos and don'ts" for parents and carers that might help you and your child survive their chronic and severe depression.

Our doctors have explained to us that there are two types of depression. One type is referred to as "cognitive" depression, which is when the depressed person is consumed with negative thoughts and beliefs. A person with cognitive depression often interprets life events in a negative way and it can become a downward spiral. These people may be able to function in society from a physical standpoint but their mental and emotional anguish makes life extremely difficult for them.

The other type of depression is called "vegetative" depression, which is when the depressed person can barely get out of bed for days, weeks or months. A person with vegetative depression cannot motivate themselves to do anything, including basic personal self-care. My child had both types of depression over a nine-year period, often to a severe degree. Both types of depression can lead to suicidal thoughts and actions.

Through this journey I have found that when a child has severe depression, there are certain things that a parent can do or say that may have a crucial impact on your child's state of mind. As the parent or carer, understanding the impact that your words and actions have on your child can make a big difference to how you and your child get through this difficult time. Having this information should help you support your child and avoid making the experience harder for them.

In this book, I have summarized what I think would be the most meaningful advice for you, as the parent, guardian or carer to a severely depressed child, teen or young adult. It includes information that I have learned from my child as well as other sources. The other sources include families dealing with mental health issues, various doctors, multiple therapists, and my own experience.

Severe depression is often accompanied by other mental health disorders such as anxiety, ADHD (attention deficit hyperactivity disorder), OCD (obsessive compulsive disorder), bipolar, personality disorders, and others. I am not trained in any of these conditions and do not address them in any detail. I have some understanding of anxiety and OCD and how they are treated, so I will make occasional references to these disorders.

Are you ready to make your child's life your top priority? You should really think about what this would mean. It means you will need to be willing to relinquish your own needs and desires at any given moment to focus on your depressed child's needs. This may get annoying and exhausting for you. You may wonder, "When do I get to do what I want to do?" You will have moments of impatience of always having to put another person's needs before your own.

Observe what is happening when you feel impatient. Maybe you were trying to get some things done and your child's needs interrupted you. Maybe you were finally taking a moment to yourself and you had to jump up to help your child. One way to get past your impatience and be in a more compassionate state of mind is to observe your child. Really see them and notice that they are struggling. Your child is not interrupting you for petty reasons. You are getting interrupted because your child truly needs help coping with life.

This level of dedication and commitment may be what is required to keep your child alive. It is not unlike when they are an infant and you would drop everything to run and save them from danger. A severely depressed child can be just as vulnerable. This may require you to change your view of your child's disorder so that you are more informed and sympathetic. You may also need to change your expectations of what you want your child to achieve in life.

In some ways, severe depression is invisible. You cannot treat it in the same way you would a physical injury and watch it heal. It is a never-ending guessing game as to what level of severity your depressed child is enduring at any particular moment. It is another challenge to know what you should do or say (or not do or not say) so that you do not worsen the situation.

If your child is in deep despair and on edge, it is more important to avoid making them feel worse than it is to try to make them feel better. This is because your child may barely register or respond to your effort to make them feel better. They will very likely, however, have a significant negative response if you do or say something that makes them feel worse. This approach goes against our urgent desire to make things better for our child. In fact, our efforts to make things better will often have the opposite effect.

We typically have a burning need to figure out why our child has severe depression. We want to know what caused it because we think that if we know what caused it, then we can solve it. Pursuing this line of thinking is likely going to go unfulfilled and will take your attention away from your child. You will probably have to accept the fact that you may never have these answers.

There will be times when caring for your child with severe depression will crush you. It can be exhausting and heartbreaking. It is emotionally draining and the stress of it could cause your own illnesses. I will provide some advice on how to manage your stress and worry.

The level of distress that a severely depressed child feels regarding seemingly simple things may baffle you. It may frustrate you. It may sadden you. You will probably feel helpless because you cannot take their suffering away.

Some of what I share may be surprising and go against your parental instincts. I am writing to the reader who wants practical advice on how to care for and respond to a child with severe depression. I am also writing to those who understand the laws of the universe and realize that our beliefs create our reality. It is sometimes a balancing act to focus on both of these fronts. I believe that we need to treat the illness that is taking place in the moment while at the same time, hold a vision of our child being well.

I cannot promise you that your severely depressed child will choose to live rather than choose to die. I can only offer my insights with my sincere intent that this book finds its way to those who need it and to those who are looking for honest and unfiltered information about how to care for a child who is suffering from this very serious and daunting mental health disorder.

I hope that that these suggestions will help you keep your child alive through their most difficult and dark days. My wish for you is that your child's terrible suffering will eventually end and that you both will be able to live a more satisfying and happy life.

As you care for your child through this experience, they will probably inspire and humble you. It takes great strength and courage for a child to live with severe depression.

CHAPTER 1

WHAT DOES YOUR CHILD'S DEPRESSION LOOK LIKE?

Your child may not look depressed yet still be suffering from severe depression. Of the two types of depression, being cognitive and vegetative, cognitive depression can be more easily camouflaged from you by your child.

Sometimes your child will find a way to go through the motions of daily life, but on the inside, they may be in deep turmoil. When people say, "They didn't seem depressed," this means that the child was very good at hiding it. Your child may have tried to talk about it to you or others at some point but were probably not fully understood or supported. Or maybe the child was embarrassed to talk about it or felt they had no one to turn to. A child can find ways to hide the severity of their depression. Hiding it takes great effort, and that makes the child's depression even worse.

I have noticed that some traits or behaviors tend to be more specific to either cognitive or vegetative depression. I am not trained in this field and these are just my own observations from my experience.

Possible signs that your child is functioning
while having cognitive depression:

- They are not interested in their birthday or other holidays.
- They are not interested in what is going on with family or friends.
- They are not interested in new things or gifts.
- Every day seems the same with no variation.
- They function with the same "I'm fine" attitude.
- There are often times when they barely talk or engage with you or others.
- Their interactions with you are either passive or irritable.
- They seem to be numb and on auto-pilot.

Possible signs that your child may have
severe vegetative depression:

- They are losing their hair.
- They are not showering or brushing their teeth.
- They withdraw from society.
- They sleep extensively for many hours or days at a time.
- They don't know or care what day it is.
- They have no interest in their life or your life.
- They have no interest in anything going on around them.
- They have no interest in things that used to interest them.
- They have no memory of specific events or conversations.

I looked at my daughter dead asleep in her bed. It was as if she was in a coma. It was the third straight day of this. And it was not for the first time. I comforted myself by saying, "Well, at least she isn't running around with bad people", "At least I know where she is" and "At least she is in her safe place and not in a hospital." During these times, I would sometimes sit beside her bed and watch my child withdraw from the world.

After saying those phrases to myself, while at the same time trying to look on the bright side, I would once again try to think of a solution. It was usually a practical solution, like trying to think of the words to encourage her to get out of bed or to think of a topic that would interest her. When I was out of the house, I would look around desperately for something that I could get for her that might make a difference. Something, anything that might put a smile on her face or get her attention.

I would wonder what mood she would be in when she woke up. I could rarely predict what it would be. It could be lethargy. It could be irritation. It could be sadness or fear. It was likely to be any emotion except joy, happiness, or contentment.

How to Respond to Their Emotions

A supportive way for you to interact with your child when they are feeling an emotion, whether depression or something else, is to empathize with them. Your child may be in varying negative moods such as anger, worry, irritability, guilt or shame. You could try agreeing with whatever they are angry about without getting angry yourself. You could try to soothe their guilt or shame about something they did or didn't do. This sharing in their emotional state will support them and make them feel noticed and validated.

Being lost in deep depression and the associated negative states is very lonely. Your child needs to feel that you are there for them so they do not feel so alone. You should not make suggestions as an attempt to get them out of the depression or negative mood, because to your child that feels like the opposite of empathizing with their feelings and making them feel less alone.

Support your child's emotions by saying phrases such as:

- "Yes, I understand that this is upsetting and it would make me mad also."
- "I agree, that is annoying."
- "Wow, you are right, that is a bizarre situation."
- "It is too bad that things like that happen."
- "I am sorry that you are going through this."
- "It is OK that you did that thing."
- "It is OK that you did not do what you wanted to do."
- "I know that depression is terrible."
- "I'm sorry that you feel bad."
- "Would you like to talk this through so that maybe you will feel a bit better about it?"

If you disagree with your child and tell them that they shouldn't be angry or guilty, they may interpret that as yet another failure on their part. Your child may tell themselves that they have the wrong emotion and reaction, yet again. Your child may also see it as you not seeing them for who they are and not noticing that they are suffering. They may think that you just want them to get better so that you can get on with your life. This translates into your child thinking that they are a burden on you, which can lead to thoughts that they may as well not be here in this life. Your child feels stuck in a terrible place and they need to know that you are there with them, sitting on the sidelines and being aware of their struggle.

The Abraham-Hicks Emotional Scale

One of the most important tools for me was understanding the Abraham-Hicks emotional scale, which I have quoted below. Information about this incredible piece of work can be found at https://www.abraham-hicks.com (© Jerry & Esther Hicks 830-755-2299).

The emotional scale may help you understand that some emotions that we perceive as negative are actually healthier than depression and higher up on the emotional scale, closer to joy. In fact, nearly every emotion has a higher and more positive energetic vibration than depression.

The Abraham-Hicks Emotional Scale

1. Joy/Appreciation/Empowered/Freedom/Love
2. Passion
3. Enthusiasm/Eagerness/Happiness
4. Optimism
5. Hopefulness
6. Contentment
7. Boredom
8. Pessimism
9. Frustration/Irritation/Impatience
10. Overwhelment
11. Disappointment
12. Doubt
13. Worry
14. Blame
15. Discouragement
16. Anger
17. Revenge

18. Hatred/Rage
19. Jealousy
20. Insecurity/Guilt/Unworthiness
21. Fear/Grief/Depression/Despair/Powerlessness

Understanding how various emotions can raise one's mood and overall energy can be very helpful. It will help you avoid inadvertently diminishing your child's experience of an emotion. Normally we may think that if our child is experiencing anger, worry or guilt, it is bad or unhealthy for them. Actually, these negative emotions may be an improvement from where they were previously.

When your child expresses irritation, anger, or any other emotion that is higher on the emotional scale than depression, let them express it. It is good that they are feeling something that is more positive than depression. Rather than trying to move them past their new emotion, you could acknowledge it and empathize so that your child can spend a bit of time feeling that emotion rather than depression.

Of course, you don't want your child to live in these negative emotions for a long time. These emotions will likely change when your child's thoughts change. Your child's negative emotion may turn back into depression or it may turn into a better emotion such as discouragement or worry. You might be able to encourage them to an emotion that is slightly higher on the emotional scale.

An example of an emotion that is an improvement over guilt and anger is boredom. If your child expresses boredom with life, it may appear to you as a troubling sign. However, boredom is much higher than depression on the emotional scale and just one step away from contentment, which can lead to hopefulness and optimism.

Remember to review the emotional scale to get a sense of where your child is on it and the nearby levels of emotions. As you watch your child and try to help them reach for an emotion that is higher on the scale, remember to be soothing and cautious. You will probably want to make suggestions to your child so that they will feel happy and joyful. These efforts will probably not work because it is difficult for a person to get to feeling happy so soon after being severely depressed. Your child may have to express other emotions along the scale such as insecurity or jealousy, before they can get to anger or worry, before they can work their way up to hopefulness and happiness. It could take days, weeks or months for a person to work their way up the emotional scale on any given subject.

Occasionally a person can jump to a higher mood if they are enthused about something or if they get in "the zone" where everything is going just right. This may be when your child is doing their "thing" which may be a talent or something they love. Sometimes, when a person comes out of the zone, they will crash down into depression. It is as if the person comes out of a pure joyful state and realizes that regular life is not nearly as thrilling as when they were excelling at their talent. This realization can be a jolt, causing them to struggle to tolerate the disappointment and mundaneness of normal life.

It may help you and your child to understand the emotional scale and to know that there is a way to work towards a more positive outlook on life. The emotional scale can be applied to any situation, thought or belief. Where you or your child are on the emotional scale will vary depending on the topic. It is OK for a person to be all over the scale, because we feel differently about different topics. The goal is to work toward a better emotion whenever you are able to do so.

How to Manage Your Mood and
Emotions During This Difficult Time

You may also be experiencing low moods and emotions due to watching your child suffer. You may be overcome with helplessness and sadness from time to time because watching your child slowly wither away feels awful.

People may tell you to go out and have fun or get away from your responsibilities. There are two likely responses to this depending on your current emotional state. You may be at a point where you can't take it anymore and you need a break. You may feel this way even though you realize that this attitude is probably not helpful to your child. Perhaps you need a break so that you can come back to your child in a more positive and supportive state of mind.

I would suggest that if you go out and leave your child, do it only if you are confident that your child will not do anything impulsive while you are gone. You should explain to your child that you are reachable if they need you. It is important that your child not feel abandoned or feel that they are a burden to you. It is essential that your child not interpret your temporary departure as your wish that you did not have to take care of them or your wish that they were not in your life.

Alternatively, you may have no desire to go out and have fun to get away from your child and your responsibilities. What other people may not understand is that you will still worry about your child even if you are away from them. Going out may not be relaxing or fun for you. It may cause more stress because you will be concerned about what your child might be doing while you are out.

You probably have not shared with others the degree of worry that you carry regarding your child. You may not have explained to anyone that you want to be with your child as much as possible because you are afraid that your child may not be here in the long term. It is OK to decline the invitations to go out. Eventually, people will stop inviting you out because they will know that you have other priorities. This may label you as anti-social and it is entirely up to you how much you share or keep private about your situation.

You should try to find ways to let the stress and worry flow through you so that you don't hold it in your body, because that can cause illness and discomfort. You should allow yourself to indulge in relaxing techniques and remember to say kind words to yourself. Gentle stretching or strenuous exercise may help reduce stress and increase circulation. There are also energy healing modalities such as qigong and reiki that can be helpful. I have used some of these methods and it has kept me functioning and healthy even during the most difficult times.

It is also important to find ways to keep yourself from being drawn into negativity during this time. Taking care of your very sick child can be emotionally exhausting and it is better for both of you if you have ways to bring yourself to a higher or happier state of mind and emotion at least some of the time. Try to remember the little things that you enjoy. Even just indulging in a small smile will lighten your mood and elevate your energy pattern.

CHAPTER 2

TOUGH LOVE DOES NOT WORK

It is hard for parents to understand why our severely depressed child finds ordinary life experiences to be so difficult. Why do they fall apart if something mildly disappointing happens? Why does one slightly negative thing ruin their whole day? Why can't they motivate themselves to do things?

You don't need to know why. You just need to accept that it is happening, know that it is devastating to your child and acknowledge that their pain is real. If you dwell on the "why" you are taking away valuable time and energy that could be spent helping them.

If you want to keep your child alive, you need to understand that their tolerance levels are not the same as yours. Comparing how you and they react to something could cause harm to both of you. It creates a situation where you are comparing yourselves and that comparison causes your child to feel guilty, inadequate and consider themselves a failure. Your child may think that they will never measure up to you or other people and the effort is too hard and impossible to achieve. This may lead to suicidal thoughts and a viewpoint that it is too hard to live life.

Instead, you need to handle your child as if they are bleeding from an open wound. You need to keep them calm and gently stop the bleeding. Don't be a hard-ass coach and tell them to get up and train through the pain. Be a kind person and tend to both their wound and their spirit.

You may need to adjust your thinking so that you can truly see that your child is in a precarious condition. If your child is also experiencing anxiety, they may be living with a gut-wrenching state of fear much of the time. It is important not to take tough love actions that you think may solve one condition because it may actually worsen both the depression and another condition that your child may have. Your child may be on a tightrope and could fall off if you push even slightly. Not to mention what could happen if you push too hard.

I knew a family where the parents literally carried their teenager into high school because the teen had been unable to force herself to go to school. The parents did this every day for several days. The parents said that after a few days of being carried into school, the teen started walking into school on her own. The parents thought they had solved their child's problem. They were so proud of themselves. They did not understand that there was a lot more going on in their child's mind than the crippling anxiety of going to school. The child also suffered from depression and being carried into school made them feel like a failure, misunderstood and unloved by their parents. This type of tough love will very likely create a lack of trust between you and your child. Your child will not trust you and will not tell you when or how they are suffering.

Embarrassing your child and making them face such a high level of stress is a terrible thing to do to them and unhealthy on many levels. It is extremely unlikely that carrying your teenager into school in front of their peers and teachers for several days

11

will solve their anxiety or depression. It is also unlikely that this treatment will result in the child suddenly becoming a functioning young adult. Much lesser versions of tough love can backfire and your child may slip further away.

Tough love actions NOT to do:

- Do not criticize your child, even in jest.
- Do not say, "You're just like your father/mother/uncle/ aunt" (whom you don't like and your child knows you don't like that person).
- Do not say, "Don't be so lazy."
- Do not force your child to get out of bed and go to school.
- Do not force your child to get up and do chores.
- Do not tell your child that you had it harder when you were a kid.
- Do not ask your child to do anything for you.
- Do not tell your child how lucky they are.
- Do not tell your child that their generation has is so easy.
- Do not punish your child for being depressed.
- Do not take away your child's phone or computer.

Keep all of these types of comments and opinions to yourself. If you really want to help your child get better, do not do or say any of these things. Even if you are thinking it. Tell other family members not to say these types of remarks to your child either. If other family members cannot respect your request, then you may need to keep those people away from your child.

It is not uncommon for the older generation to want to apply tough love and criticize your child because they think it will turn them into a strong functioning adult. These people will probably also criticize you as being too soft and coddling your child. Do not let your child hear these negative comments that are directed towards you. Your child will feel bad and guilty that you are being criticized by others, due to their illness and you having to take care of them. Your child will feel helpless to protect you and may think that the only way they can make things better for you is to not be in your life.

Don't yell at your child to "Smarten up and get out of bed" or say things like, "What is wrong with you?!" Maybe when you were young, having your parent yell at you worked. Maybe you were actually just being lazy. Your severely depressed child is not being lazy.

Something is wrong. Your child is sick. They are stuck and cannot find a way out. Yelling at your child will make them feel scared and alone. Your child may not want to live that way or live with you. They may feel that their home is unsafe as long as they are living with you and relying on you. Your child may want to get away but have no way to do so. Except the permanent way.

Remind yourself that this is not a competition about who had the hardest childhood. Nor is there an easy fix. Your gut reaction may be to get your child functioning again quickly so that you don't have to look at what is really going on. You may be trying to quell your own pain from seeing your child suffer. Your brain is telling you that if you can just fix it, then it will all go away and everyone will feel better. It would be better if you change this thought process and instead, really look at what is going on.

Your child isn't choosing not to function. They actually wish that they could live their life like other people. They want to have interests and enjoyment in life. They aren't choosing to lay around in bed. The fact is, when they are in this condition, living life is nearly too much for them to bear. Your child is just trying to hang on and barely hoping that things will get better.

The human spirit is strong. There are countless stories of people who overcame hardship. Your severely depressed child isn't avoiding living their life due to hardship. Severe depression is a clinical condition where the brain cannot produce the chemicals that generate motivation, interest, joy or excitement. It is a deep, dark hole that is suffocating. If your child was lost in a deep, dark hole, you would not tell them to dance and look on the bright side because when you were little you were in a deeper, darker hole and you turned out fine.

We are supposed to want a better life for our children than how we grew up. It is not a competition of which generation had it worse. It will just make your child feel bad to know that you think they are not as strong as you are.

I knew a parent who was stuck on the thought that she herself grew up in difficulty and learned early how to take care of herself. This mother couldn't understand that if she was very strong and capable at an early age, why wasn't her teen the same way? This mother would say these remarks repeatedly to herself and in front of her child. Maybe the parent truly couldn't understand why her child was so incapable of living life. Or maybe the parent thought or hoped that this talk would inspire her child to do better. This type of talk is not inspiring to a severely depressed child, it just makes them feel worse about themselves.

Just because you may not understand why your child is like this or have any real appreciation for how bad your child is suffering, doesn't mean it isn't true. I am telling you that their condition is real and you cannot bully them out of it.

14

Some viewpoints that you need to accept:

- Your view of life is not the same as your child's.
- Your opinion for how your child should get out of depression will not work, or it would have already.
- Your reaction to things is not the same as your child's.
- Accept that you should not give your child advice on how to function.
- Accept that your child is sick and that life is very difficult for them.
- Accept that this is your child's life, at least for now.
- Accept that this is your life.
- Accept that you are the parent of a child who has a serious mental health disorder.

Do you love your child and want to help them get well? Or do you want to toughen your child up by giving them a difficult life so that they will endure and overcome it? Your child already has a difficult life. The difficulty your child is experiencing is not comparable to the difficult life events that you may have had.

Unless you have experienced severe depression yourself, you cannot imagine how scary and suffocating it is. Severe clinical depression is a mental disorder that is not caused by an event or several events. Some events can certainly make a person feel somewhat depressed. We have probably all experienced temporary depression after an upsetting life event. That type of temporary depression is not what your child is experiencing. Your child is experiencing something much worse.

Your child is sick. Our role as parents is to help them get well. We should nurse our child back to health, not to whip them into doing what we want them to do. Your child's pain may manifest in another way if you apply tough love. It may manifest in a worse way than not going to school or not getting out of bed.

CHAPTER 3

ALWAYS SHOW YOUR CHILD THAT YOU CARE

We assume as parents that our children know that we love them. However, if your child is telling themselves hundreds of times a minute and thousands of times a day that they are unworthy to live their life, they become insecure and uncertain if you love them. In fact, they often convince themselves that you do not love them. Your child may believe that they are not lovable or worthy of love.

Your severely depressed child carries a lot of guilt for being a burden to their parents and they will need to hear you say that you love them on a regular basis. They depend on hearing it. When your child does not hear you say that you love them, they may interpret that to mean that you must not love them anymore.

Try to make saying "I love you" part of your day, several times a day. You could also give your child a specific compliment, but don't be overly enthusiastic. If you are too enthusiastic it will put pressure on your child to keep performing and succeeding at whatever you complimented them on. Your child may feel that it is impossible to keep succeeding and that can be too much pressure to live with. Their belief and anticipation of their impending failure will become even more crushing than it already is.

Finding this balance of expressing your genuine love for your child throughout the day and also holding back the full weight of your encouragement may be difficult for you as a parent. The reality is that you will have many days and weeks to practice this. The appropriate balance may vary from day to day.

Examples of small compliments that are not overly enthusiastic:

- "You got your phone cord untangled, that's good."
- "You spent time with your cat/dog/pet, I bet they liked that."
- "You found a new site for (insert their latest interest), that was a good discovery."
- Tell your child that they are strong to endure such depression.
- Tell your child that they are brave to keep going.
- Tell your child that they have amazing fortitude to keep looking for hope.
- Tell your child that you admire their strength.
- Tell your child that you know it is very hard to live when it feels so bad.
- Remind your child of some of their positive traits.
- Tell your child that you are glad that they are in your life.
- Thank your child for being here with you.

Reassure and support your child with comments such as:

- Tell your child that you will take care of them as long as you live if it comes to that.
- Tell your child that you will make other arrangements for their care if needed.

- Tell your child that you know their pain is real.
- Tell your child that their condition does not mean they are a bad person.
- Tell your child that depression is an experience that they may just have to get through until it changes for the better.
- Tell your child that it will not always be this bad.
- Tell your child that they are not a failure.
- Tell your child that they are a good person.
- Tell your child that they are not alone.
- Tell your child that you always love them and support them even when you have disagreements.

If your child has been in bed for days, weeks or months, there may be a point where they have body odor or bad breath. This is actually relatively common with severely depressed people. Instead of being upset if this happens to your child, it is better to change your attitude and see this as a phase that your child is going through. Your child wasn't always like this so there is a good chance that they will not always be like this.

Do not mention anything about your child's lack of hygiene or ask if they have washed recently. Do not encourage your child to shower or brush their teeth and do not discuss ways to make the task easier. Saying these things will have a negative impact on your child's mood and mental state. These comments are not perceived as encouragement. Your child will perceive these comments as pointing out their failure. Your child is well aware of the fact that they have not washed in a long time. Your child does not enjoy being dirty. There is absolutely no good reason for you to bring it up.

If your child has other mental health disorders in addition to depression, the uncleanliness could make those conditions worse. Your child's mind may be on a loop where they cannot figure out how to clean themselves in a way that does not create several other problems along each step. This problem solving can be exhausting for them. It is easier on your child's mind to just stay unclean than to climb that mountain of mental strain. They know that by not cleaning, it just makes everything worse. Your child feels trapped and feels that they will never get free. Your child feels like a failure because they cannot do this one simple thing that they used to be able to do and that everyone else can do.

When your child does manage to shower or do another thing that they haven't been able to do in a long time, you should not point it out. A person would think that a child would want you to notice their accomplishment, particularly if you understand how hard it was for them. But your depressed child does not want you to compliment their success or even mention it. This is because your child does not know when or if they will be able to undertake that task again. You should just act as if nothing has changed and continue being supportive.

If your child chooses to mention their accomplishment, then of course, you should acknowledge it. You could say that you noticed that they did something that was difficult. You should tell your child that it is a positive step forward and that you understand that by accomplishing that thing once does not necessarily mean that they will be able to do it again right away. Reassure them that you do not have any expectations nor do think that they are all better.

This approach may go against your parental urges and natural inclination. You may think that if you say it is OK for your child to not take care of themselves, that you are giving them permission to do just that. You may also think that by saying this, it might encourage your child to give up trying.

You will probably feel the need to praise and encourage your child. You may think that positive cheerleading will lead to success. You must hold back from these urges. Your child's depressed mind is not functioning in a way where they perceive encouragement as a positive. If your child shows improvement in any area, do not cheer their accomplishment or express any new expectations.

One form of motivation that is not praise, is to set up a rewards chart. This is a chart where the child earns a small amount of money for every time they brush their teeth or shower or accomplish other similar self-care tasks. You should only do this with your child's agreement. The idea is that it will motivate your child's brain so that they can push past the negative thought loops to enable them to accomplish some of these goals.

This type of rewards chart is not the same as an allowance or chore chart. This is an actual tool that mental health professionals sometimes suggest. Your child will not get rich from this and making money is not the incentive or objective. This tool is intended to generate in the depressed person's brain a sense of accomplishment by working and earning. It acknowledges that these tasks are actual work and take effort and therefore should be rewarded. There may be some weeks when this is successful and there may be weeks when it does not motivate your child. This rewards chart is a short-term tool and not intended to be used long term. It will either work or it won't. If it doesn't work or stops working, you should just take the chart down and not dwell on it.

You could try to come up with other motivational tools with your child. Maybe go out for a treat after an accomplishment. The rewards should be simple and serve as a bonus to their daily life. The rewards should not be linked to daily needs that are critical to your child's comfort, such as their phone or computer time.

If your child is able and willing to identify types of motivational rewards, it may be a positive endeavor. However, if the tools do not work, your child may see it as yet another failure on their part. You may conclude that it is better not to pursue this line of treatment. This may be another balancing act that you will have to learn to navigate.

CHAPTER 4

GIVE UP ON SOCIETY'S EXPECTATIONS

People may say or imply that your child is lazy or privileged. People may say that you are spoiling them. People may judge you and your child because you do not fit in with society norms. People may ask questions such as, "Are you are getting your child help?" or "Are they on medication?"

People may have the opinion that all your child needs is a purpose in life. They may also insist that you need to get your child outside to get some sun or take vitamin D. Many people believe that it must just be the cloudy weather or winter season causing your child's depression. Some people may imply that you must not be doing enough or you are not doing it right.

When people make these comments, you may try to defend yourself or your child. You may try to explain the situation to these people or try to educate the person talking to you. You will likely get very tired of doing this. You may begin to not speak of it at all. It can be a very private pain that you are going through. If you have family members that do not understand, that can make it even harder.

Having to explain why your child does not attend family

events, participate in birthdays or holidays and does not experience the same milestones that other children and teens have can be difficult and painful. Do you make excuses? Or do you just say that your child "…is severely depressed in bed, and yes, we are getting treatment and no, I don't want to talk about it." Of course, the right answer in the right situation is rarely this straightforward.

My daughter said to me, "If I were in the hospital sick with cancer people would understand and be sympathetic." She was often frustrated with people who do not understand that mental illness is a real thing. She always encouraged me to tell anyone about her condition. I tended to keep it private to protect her and myself from judgement. But my child wanted people to know so that it would become less of a stigmatized topic. Thankfully, mental health issues are much more accepted today and talked about more openly than they were in the past.

We all hold belief systems that we live by. Some beliefs are obvious, such as, "If you work hard you will succeed." Other beliefs are subconscious or subtle such as those that trigger an automatic physical or emotional reaction. Some beliefs are positive, like when you smile at a fond memory. Others are negative, such as when we clench our teeth or get a bad feeling in the pit of our stomach when we hear upsetting news or when we don't like something.

Your experience of taking care of your severely depressed child will cause you to re-evaluate your beliefs and priorities. Giving up on the expectations of society and becoming aware of our stubborn belief systems, particularly when they are centered around what we think our child should accomplish in life, will make room for a new attitude that will be more supportive to your child.

This release of trying to meet society's expectations and becoming more aware and flexible to change your beliefs will help both you and your child. The release of your own dreams and goals for your child will allow you to be more focused on the one main objective, which is to keep your child alive which includes accepting them for who they are.

Society norms and parental expectations that you may have to let go of, at least temporarily:

- Let go of expecting your child to attend school.
- Let go of your desire for your child to have friends.
- Let go of your need to see your child socialize with family.
- Let go of your need for your child to take care of their personal hygiene.
- Let go of your expectation that your child will be able to live on their own.
- Let go of your dream for your child to exercise or join a sport.
- Let go of the idea that your child will have a "normal" life.
- Let go of your expectation that your child will graduate high school.
- Let go of your expectation that your child will have a romantic relationship.
- Let go of your dream of your child getting a job or having a career.
- Let go of your anticipation of your child getting a driver's license.
- Let go of your vision that your child will become a functioning adult.
- Let go of expecting your child to be an active participant in your life or the family unit.

It can be difficult to function in your life feeling normal or happy when you think your child is slowly dying at home in bed. It can be hard to focus on work, other family members and your other responsibilities.

I would try my best not to leave my daughter home alone for more than three consecutive hours. This was partly due to my worry generally and partly due to the fact that if she woke up alone, she may be in a severe state of distress and be crying out for me. I did not want to cause her this agony and sometimes I worried that she would hurt herself. The hurt would not necessarily be physical harm (she and I had discussed that) but it could be mental and emotional harm. My child might tell herself that she was alone and unloved and unworthy and bad. She might tell herself this over and over again until I could get home to reassure her that I loved her and she was not alone and that she is worthy and that she is a good person.

It was just as likely is that my child would wake up in her regular state of being deeply depressed and lethargic. I would text her and ask if I could bring her favorite food or beverage home as a treat. Sometimes she would say yes and tell me what she wanted. Sometimes she didn't answer because she was sleeping. Other times she said it didn't matter, and that she did not want anything. Sometimes she would beg me to come home and other times she would say I could stay out as long as I wanted. It was almost always a crushing blow to my heart.

When the situation gets to this point, you probably just want any improvement at all, no matter how small. You will truly change your expectations. You will no longer be focused on your child going to school, talking with friends, having a job or getting their driver's license. You will just be hoping that a favorite food, a cute toy or fun item will perk them up just a little bit for just a moment.

It can sometimes be a stretch of your mind and spirit to treat your child's illness that is in front of you while at the same time trying to hold the positive vision of them getting better. One way to bridge this gap is to hold a closer vision, a vision of them getting slightly better rather than being fully well. Try to hold some hope even while you are coping with their current terrible condition.

Some things you should NOT do:

- Don't push against the situation.
- Don't pretend that it isn't that bad.
- Don't blame it on social media.
- Don't blame it on yourself or family genetics.
- Don't blame it on their other parent.
- Don't put your life on hold indefinitely.
- Don't give up hope that your child's condition will improve.

Some things you may need to do:

- Find a way to live your life in your primary role as the carer to your sick child.
- Find a way to work other things into your primary role.
- Find a way to manage your stress and worry.
- Dig deep to access the patience you will need to endure this experience.
- Mourn the loss of having a healthy and self-sufficient child.
- Keep an open mind that your child will get better.

Alternatives to Normal Societal Milestones

Train yourself out of having society's expectations and try to see other options for your child. Maybe your child will not finish high school but will eventually pass a high school equivalency test that will enable them to get a job or into adult classes at a trade school, college or university.

Maybe your child will not go to any additional school but will be able to get a job that gives them a sense of accomplishment and they will be able to earn a living. Maybe your child will make friends at their job and learn valuable life skills.

Maybe your child will not get their driver's license but will learn how to navigate other forms of transportation. Maybe your child will not have a romantic relationship but they will make friends or become a leader or member of a group.

The point is to release your own and society's beliefs and expectations so that you can see alternate paths for your child to get better and re-enter society in whatever form it comes.

Your child getting better may look different depending on the severity of their depression. Getting better may be your child getting out of bed and showering on a regular basis. It might be your child noticing other people and pets in the household and asking about their wellbeing. Getting better may be your child caring about the current date, holidays, news or events. It may be deciding that they want to live even though they see their entire future as being severely depressed and dependent on others.

Your Heart and Mind

You will get used to not having 100% of your mental or emotional strength at your disposal. Part of your awareness may always be thinking about your sick child and trying to find a solution or come up with a way to help.

There is a philosophy right now that says, "Put yourself first." There is a lot of promotion of self-care. I agree that there is validity to this philosophy and you have to take care of yourself as well as your child. However, in the moments when your child's life may be on the line, you will need to put their care first.

You won't always be putting your child first. Later, as your child gets better and they have an awareness of other people in the family, you will be able to establish a better balance among other family members and yourself.

You need to try to find a way to live your life as best you can without being overcome with guilt, worry and stress. There may be times when you are exhausted from tip-toeing around your child's pain and hurt feelings. Maybe you will say something harsh because you are at the end of your rope. This may cause you to feel regretful and guilty. Remind yourself that you are doing the best you can from where you are in that moment and that you are always trying to do better. You need to try to find a way to be at peace with your constant state of taking care of your child so that you can find a way focus on your work and other responsibilities when you need to.

You will get used to your child not responding to your efforts of trying to cheer them up. Don't let the repeated disappointment of your failed efforts shatter your heart. This is just a journey for both of you. The situation will eventually change because everything is in a constant state of flux. You just need to carry on until the situation changes for the better.

CHAPTER 5

HOW YOU CAN CHANGE YOURSELF TO BE MORE HELPFUL TO YOUR CHILD

As you take care of your child with severe depression, you will likely need to change your approach to problem solving. This will challenge your belief systems and how you operate. This process of changing to be more open minded and positive will help you as well as your child, because you will start to see your own biases and stubborn beliefs.

One stubborn belief of yours might be to look for a cause for your child's depression so that you can assign blame or so you can fix it. This effort might have some benefit if your child is just suffering from normal depression caused by a specific event, such as a death in the family or bullying. We have all probably experienced this type of temporary depression at some point in our lives. Sometimes treating the memory of a trauma and its repercussions can be helpful. If your child knows of a trauma that is causing them distress, then of course, this may need to be talked through and treated with professional help.

Severe debilitating depression does not necessarily have a direct link to a particular trauma. Instead of trying to identify the cause of your child's severe depression and chasing after that, you may need to accept that your child is having this challenging experience and just embrace your role as their carer to see them through it.

If you focus on finding a cause for your child's severe depression, it may not help your child and may actually cause harm. A severely depressed child does not want to talk about trauma or potential trauma because that is depressing to talk about. They cannot bear any activity, such as a depressing discussion with you, that creates more depression.

Even if you did find a cause or multiple causes for your child's severe depression, those events cannot be undone. You cannot change the past and this search takes your attention away from where it is truly needed, which is to comfort and support your child. Your child's sessions with a psychologist or counsellor can address specific causes and events if needed, while you focus on being your child's trusted supporter.

Don't dwell on finding a cause for the depression:

- Don't search for a past trauma.
- Finding a potential cause will not likely enable you to fix it.
- Your child does not want to re-live a trauma.
- Your child does not want to remember a forgotten trauma.
- Your child does not care if there was trauma, they just want to feel better.
- Address the current reality not a past possibility.
- Look to the future and not the past.
- Don't subject your child to your effort to find a cause.

- Don't subject your child to your worry that something bad must have happened to them.
- Don't subject your child to your self-blame of thinking that maybe you let something bad happen to them.

Identifying a trauma or event is more about you wanting to find a cause for your child's depression so that you can fix it. You may feel a need to identify a cause so that you can have a place to lay blame. Maybe you think you will feel better once you know there is a reason for your child's suffering. Perhaps it would allow you to relieve your guilt as to whether you did or did not have a role in your child's possible trauma.

Your severely depressed child most likely does not care if a trauma caused their severe depression or not. They likely view trauma as an event that is in the past and therefore cannot be changed. They are in pain in the here and now. What your child wants and needs from you is your love, attention, and support to just get through the day.

It may make you feel better to find a cause and blame the perpetrator. Or maybe if you can determine that it was a random event that you could not control, you will feel less guilty. Regardless of how you comfort yourself, you need to remember that your priority at this critical time is to help your child and keep them alive.

Be Observant

Pay attention to your child's patterns. You will then be able to adjust your patterns around theirs. This means that you will be changing a lot about how you think and operate.

Learn how to be aware of your child's state of being:

- Be watchful (without staring) of your child's facial expressions.
- Be watchful of your child's body language.
- Notice their patterns: when they eat, when they sleep, when they go to the washroom or move from room to room.
- Notice if they are behind closed doors for a longer than typical time period.
- Notice if they randomly start looking through their stuff.
- Notice if they are talking in chat groups.
- Notice if they slip into child-like patterns or emotional states.
- Notice if they act more adult or in charge of aspects of their life.

As you become more aware of your child's state of mind you will be better able to interact with them in a helpful way. If your child is showing an interest in their belongings, they may be having a bit of energy and want to reconnect with a something they care about. You could ask your child what they are wanting to do and you may be able to assist if they can't find something.

If your child fluctuates between grown up behaviors and child-like patterns, it may be an indication of their confidence level in that moment. If your child is acting more capable, they may be feeling a bit better and want to accomplish something. If they are acting more childlike, they may be feeling overwhelmed or insecure, and need to be taken care of.

You also need to be aware of your own actions. Do you discuss your to-do list for the next day on the current day? Sometimes hearing your task list can be stressful to your child.

They know that you have other responsibilities and that it is hard on you to have a sick child to take care of. This may make them feel bad about themselves and unworthy or guilty. You could either keep silent about your daily plans in front of your child, or speak of your tasks positively and explain how you can fit them around your primary desire to take care of your child.

Do you voice your own random thoughts while driving in the car with your child or when you are together around the house? You may need to start being quiet. Stop talking about what is on your busy mind. Talking about your own random thoughts and opinions can be upsetting to your child. Learning to talk less will have the side benefit of quieting your mind so that you can be more present in the moment. You will be getting one of the benefits of meditation without having to set aside the time to meditate. You being quiet also allows you to notice your child's patterns more accurately. It will also provide an opening for your child to speak and share their thoughts.

Don't assume anything about:

- What your child is thinking.
- What your child is feeling.
- What may have happened to your child.
- Your child's outer condition.
- Your child's inner condition.
- Your child's concerns of the moment.
- Your child's concerns of the day.

You do not know what your child is really thinking about until they share it with you. They may be having thoughts that surprise and baffle you. When your child starts to share their thoughts with you, you need to be non-judgmental and keep a calm demeanor. Speak in a calm voice and ask them to tell you more about it.

Your child may be having bad and disturbing dreams. They may be dreaming about war, death, abuse or torture. Your child might be dreaming these things about themselves, other people or animals. If your child keeps these dreams to themselves, they may dwell on the upsetting images. This will likely be distressing for your child. You can encourage your child to tell you about their dreams and talk about what they may mean. Remind your child that dreams are not literal representations of what may happen in life. Dreams are full of symbolism and when a person is depressed, dreams can often reflect one's fears or other negative thought patterns.

Your child may be watching world events that are upsetting. They may feel helpless when they hear about the wars and environmental conditions. Your child may have the view that there is no real future for their generation. It is hard for many young people today to have hope or to plan for a future when they view the world as being in a dire condition. You could encourage your child to research some of the positive things that people are doing to help the environment and change the political climate. Many young people are making a real difference to improve the world condition.

Being able to discuss what is on their mind with you, without fear of judgement, will help your child open up even more. It will build trust between you. Being able to talk about what is on their mind is helpful for your child. It is also better for your child to know that they can talk to you about anything than for them to reach out to a stranger.

This trust and open communication with you may lead your child to finding the strength to do an activity that they had been unable to do. Now that they have talked through what was on their mind, their mind has the space to pursue something different. This is a very precarious time and you should resist your urge to show your happiness about their new found activity and you should not encourage them to do more.

Don't mention:

- If your child is having a better day, don't point it out.
- If your child shows an improvement, don't assume everything is all better.
- If your child manages a big goal, don't expect it to happen again.
- Don't discuss food or eating habits.
- Assuming that your child does not have an eating disorder, let them eat what they want.
- Don't mention how long your child has been on their computer or phone.
- Don't assume all social media is bad. Sometimes it provides a much-needed distraction from your child's emotional pain.
- Don't mention body odor or ailments.
- Don't ask your child a lot of questions or ask them to make a lot of choices.
- Don't mention that people were asking why your child did not attend an event.

Do mention:

- Invite your child to share with you what they are reading/ watching/learning.
- Do mention your child's positive traits.
- Suggest that you might buy a specific favorite food or beverage.

- Acknowledge and thank your child when they teach you something that you didn't know. It may be about a new subject, social media drama, or how to use an application on your phone.
- Do mention that someone wished your child well, when people ask you how they are doing.
- Remind family members to please send a birthday gift and tell your child when a gift has arrived. You do not have to save the gift for the actual birthday, especially if it could raise your child's spirits to have it when it arrives.

Your child may be afraid to show improvement if you start expecting things from them or if you treat them as if the depression is over. They need the safety and security of being able to make small improvements and still be cared for as a severely depressed person.

Getting out of depression takes many small steps and there will likely be setbacks. Your child needs to know that you understand that if they make a small improvement it does not mean that they are suddenly well or that they will be able to do it again. They also need to know that if they make one small improvement that you are not going to assume they are all better and leave them alone to go tend to your own matters.

Eating Habits

I believe that it is very important that you not spend time discussing your child's eating habits or their body weight when they are suffering from severe depression. You just want to be sure that your child is eating and staying hydrated. At this point it matters less what they are eating, as long as they are eating. You don't want to add food guilt, body hatred or body dysmorphia to their depressed condition.

You should probably let your child eat what they want, as long as it is not actually harmful. You could try to encourage them to eat something specific or provide their favorite foods. But in the end, it matters less about what they are eating and more about letting them eat whatever makes them feel better.

Of course, you don't want your child to develop an unhealthy eating pattern or eating disorder.

If your child is currently eating too little, too much or binge eating, then they may have an eating disorder. If you have any concern that your child may have an eating disorder, then you should seek professional treatment right away. Some eating disorders require hospitalization and can lead to death.

The human body can survive on nearly any food intake. During this time of your child's severe depression, you are trying to keep your child alive, not put them on a specific dietary regimen to achieve some sort of weight goal that you believe is important. If all your child wants to eat is sweets or processed foods, let them. As long as they are eating. Eventually their body will yearn for something else and probably something healthier. In the meantime, it is best not to bother your child about their food intake or body condition.

Faith, Spirituality, the Law of Attraction and Quantum Physics

You may find comfort in your faith, your form of spirituality or your understanding of scientific universal laws. This topic spans many different cultures and philosophies and it may be helpful for you to be open minded to learning about various beliefs.

You might turn to these areas for answers to your questions.

A review of different belief systems may take the edge off some of the emotional pain that you and your child are going through and give you both some comfort. Whatever belief you turn to, keep in mind that it should offer hope and positivity and not be too rigid. You need to have the freedom to pursue various treatment options for your child.

Some spiritual perspectives suggest that a person may choose a specific difficult experience in life so that they learn something or so the people around them may learn something. If that is the case, then maybe you have to allow your child to experience the severe depression so that they, and the people most affected, can learn from it and then then move past it.

Various spiritual teachers say that severe depression may be an agreement your child made on some level to come here and experience. Maybe your child is on some sort of pre-destined journey to experience suffering. Maybe it was some sort of life plan or soul contract or has to do with a past or alternate life. These teachers also point out that we all have the ability to change the scope and scale of our life plan with our free will. Maybe you and your child can narrow the scope or shorten the duration of this experience.

Many scholars have explained the relationship between the law of attraction and quantum physics. Countless books discuss this principle and there are many people choosing to consciously follow these principles to manifest what they want their life experience to be. This is the idea that one's thoughts and beliefs bring more of the same. Even when one understands these principles it can be challenging to manifest health and wellness for your child, particularly when you have to address the reality of the illness that is right in front of you.

Intuitive guides and channelers sometimes explain depression or anxiety as when a person is disconnected from their source energy. Source energy is explained as the life force of the universe. Different faiths refer to it as their form of deity. Various healing modalities use words such as "chi" or "prana". Some people refer to it as "being in the zone."

Some teachers explain that anxiety and depression is caused when we are not keeping up with our momentum. They say that a person can get so connected to source energy and generate so much momentum for their future manifestation, that when the person gets disconnected, the pain from that disconnection is severe and much more intolerable than it is for other people. That disconnection can cause fear, anxiety and depression.

Spiritual teachers have said that we all have the ability to feel other people's energy as well as the mass consciousness. Many young people today are more intuitive than previous generations. These young people are more empathetic and are more aware of the extra-sensory abilities that are available to them. The reality of wars and other bad things in our world truly cause them distress because they can feel the pain and suffering very strongly and clearly. It may be helpful for your child to learn how to differentiate between their own energy and that of others. This is not to remove their empathy or compassion for those who are suffering, but rather to enable your child to have the awareness of others without having to feel the suffering so directly.

You may wonder if your child's severe depression experience is because their purpose in life is to only be here for a short time. Some spiritual teachers and religious leaders say that that is what happens when a miscarriage occurs or when a baby or child dies young.

If any of this is true, what happens if your child gets through the worst of the severe depression? You may have a new round of questions. You may wonder if your child is going to stay on

40

their path of having a short life or will they live a long life? Will your child become disinterested in living life or will they succeed to fulfill their dreams? Did your child learn what they needed to learn from their life and now they are done? Will your child move on to have another challenging experience or will their life get easier and more enjoyable? Of course, as parents we hope that the answer is in the positive.

Regardless of your faith or belief systems, perhaps it will give you some comfort if you can view your child's severe depression experience as an agreed upon journey. A journey between you and your child, where you are in the role of their carer. This perspective is healthier than thinking of yourself as a failure as a parent or trying to find a reason for your child's illness. Thinking negative thoughts about yourself or the situation is not helpful. Learning to accept the journey is more empowering. This acceptance, in tandem with you holding the faith or a vision of your child in better health, is a positive framework from which to operate.

If you can maintain a belief that the severe depression will eventually end and also be open to discussing various spiritual and scientific viewpoints, it may be helpful to both you and your child. Your child's recovery may happen suddenly or it may happen little by little over a longer period of time. There will probably be no single spiritual or medical explanation.

Try to have some sort of positive outlook:

- Decide to live fully and embrace your role as the carer to your child.
- Appreciate the time you have with your child.
- Stop wishing it was different.
- Stop wishing you could find the solution.

- Accept that your child has a different role to play in the family unit.
- See it as an experience that you have agreed to undertake.
- Value the closeness that it can bring between you and your child.

You may never understand why your child has severe depression. Ultimately, that doesn't matter. You have to accept it. You may have to give up your own desires in any given moment to put their needs first. It is easier if you can embrace your role in life right now as being your child's support system and adjust your own personal goals around that.

One of the most important things that you can say and do for your child is to tell them you love them and make sure that there will always be support systems that they can count on throughout their life.

CHAPTER 6

HOW TO INTERRUPT YOUR CHILD'S SUFFOCATING DEPRESSIVE THOUGHT PATTERNS

Your child may have cognitive depression which can mean that they have thousands of self-critical thoughts racing through their mind on a loop. Alternatively, your child may have vegetative depression where they do not have the mental energy or emotional motivation to get out of bed. Their mind may be numb or sluggish with negative thoughts.

You do not want to add your busy thoughts and daily issues to your child's self-hatred and guilt. You could try to gently pause your child's negative thought loop by introducing a new thought or topic that peaks your child's interest enough to get their attention. This may temporarily interrupt their repetitive negative thoughts.

You could ask a question or mention something minor to your child. Your child may react with annoyance because you have interrupted their thought loop that they were focused upon. Now you are distracting them and that may be irritating to your child. This effort is most effective if you are asking about something that is relevant to your child. You don't want to ask a lot of questions that require effort for them to answer or too many choices for them to consider. Simple questions or comments that encourage a response are best.

You may need to do this if your child has been isolated in their bedroom or another room for too long. Don't call out loudly in a way that startles them or that they could interpret as being judgmental. You don't want your child to think that they have been caught doing something bad or wrong. Your child may already be on edge and the adrenalin that comes from fear and anxiety can be damaging to them. It is best to be a supportive voice and not a parent who is trying to find out what they are doing. Speak in a kind and quiet voice and say comments such as, "I'm just checking on you to see if I can help you with anything" or "Would you be able to come out and look at this toy I got for your pet?" Try to lead their attention to coming out of the room to do something else.

You could say, "Would you like something to eat?" Suggest two or three options, no more. This may engage your child in a conversation that is not too overwhelming because you are giving your child just a few options rather an open-ended question for them to suggest what they may want to eat. If your child is in despair they may not be able to think of anything they want if you ask an open-ended question. If you offer two or three options, and they don't like any of the options you have suggested, their mind may engage and they may suggest something else.

It may take multiple tries before you notice that you are able to interrupt their internal repetitive thoughts. I suggest that you try it every so often but not constantly. It is a delicate balance to do it when you see that your child is deep into their internal thoughts yet not so often that they perceive it as nagging.

Sometimes your child will not realize that you have attempted a conversation several times that day. They may not remember what conversation the two of you had recently. It matters less about what you are discussing than the fact that they are interacting with you instead of listening to their repetitive negative thoughts.

Gentle things to ask or comment on to pause
your child's negative thought loop:

- "I like the (item of clothing) that you chose to wear today."
- "Can I get you this or that (name one or two specific items) to eat (or drink)?"
- "I will get you a (mention their favorite snack) if you want one."
- "How about I move this item out of your way so you can walk around your room easier?"
- "Did you notice that your pet is being playful today?"
- "I'm here if you need me."
- "I am happy to discuss anything that you want to talk about."
- "I love you and understand that you are having a difficult time."
- Ask your child if they have any new ideas about their latest interest (i.e. the show they are watching, tattoos or piercings that they are considering, computer games they are playing, or fan fiction they are reading).
- "May I help you with anything?"
- "Would you tell me what you are thinking about?"

Topics not to comment on:

- Don't talk about all the tasks that you have to do today. It may make your child feel guilty that they are not helping. They will be sad that you have a hard life and they are a burden on you.
- Don't list a bunch of activities that your child could do when they get better. It may make them feel even worse about how the depression is wasting their life.
- Don't get frustrated and sigh or groan when they don't respond or if they respond negatively.
- Don't mention what other people or their peers are doing.
- Keep the fact that their depression is crushing you to yourself.
- Don't say that you are having a bad day.
- Don't express your low feelings.

The fact is, it is hard for your child to care about anything or anyone else when they are severely depressed. The negative thought loop is loud in their head and taking up all of their attention. Nothing else is particularly interesting or important to your child. If you point out that you are struggling also, that will add to your child's guilt and their feelings of being a burden. They will also feel bad for you and that adds to their long list of negative feelings.

Topics That Your Child Might be Interested in Discussing with You

Your child is extremely sad and may have no interest in anything. Try to figure out what few things might still hold an interest to them. It won't be the normal things like going to school, learning to drive or getting a job. It might be something their pet is doing or the idea of getting a new blanket or pillow for their bed. It may be a different topic at any given time.

Scents can affect or trigger a person's emotions. Your child may or may not be interested in this. You could ask them to smell different candle options and then light one. Of course, you should teach them where to put the candle so that it is not a fire hazard, if they do not already understand how to do this. You should check on the candle on a regular basis because your child may or may not remember to blow it out before they fall asleep. You could also consider air freshener or discuss perfume or body sprays as something to talk about or for your child to sniff or try out. Be watchful of your child's reaction to this discussion because you don't want them to interpret it as a judgement about their personal hygiene.

Music can also affect a person's emotions. This is most helpful if you know what emotion a specific piece of music might cause in your child. You don't want to inadvertently trigger a bad memory or emotion. Positive examples might be holiday music that they enjoyed when they were younger and happier. It may be the current music in the genre they prefer. Maybe gentle background music coming from another room will stimulate a better emotion for them. You should be watchful and notice if the music is causing sad or regretful feelings that may worsen your child's depression.

Your child might be interested in talking about a loved one, pet or friend who passed away. You should be willing to talk about that pet or loved one. It may make your child sad or it may engage them. It depends on a number of factors. You won't know until you try. Even if your child does not want to talk about that person in the moment, you are showing them that you are open to discuss the matter. Your child may respond to your suggestion of making a scrapbook of photos and memories of the pet or loved one. Your child may come to you later to talk about the person or death in general.

If the person who died had ended their own life, your child may or may not be interested in hearing about it. Your child has probably thought about ending their own life and may be curious about what happened and how the family is handling it. Even if you are apprehensive that such a conversation might make your child think about suicide, avoiding the topic will not necessarily prevent your child from thinking about it. Having this discussion will demonstrate to your child that you are willing to discuss anything with them and it may encourage them to come to you when a serious topic is on their mind.

I know a child whose mother died when the child was young. The child spent years telling herself that her mother would be mad at her and disappointed in the person she was becoming. The child, who was now a teenager, thought her mother would be mad about various failures that the teen viewed about herself. I had received a strong feeling urging me to find the teen and talk to her about her mother. I told her that I believed that her mother was proud of her and loved her always. The teen smiled and showed a glimmer of hope in her eyes. You would think that a child or teen would know this already and not need to hear it. Actually, depressed children, teens and young adults need to be reminded that they are loved.

If you see a flash of hope in your child's eyes when discussing a topic, you could gently pursue that topic from time to time. Over time, that specific interest may wane and be replaced with something else. You can use that first topic to lead to other similar topics that may also interest your child. It is like following the breadcrumbs from one topic to another to stay on a course that your child may find soothing or interesting. This trail can change depending on the day or the moment.

The severe depression will cause your child to go back to their negative thought process even if they have had a discussion with you that temporarily distracted them from their pain. You can watch their facial expressions and you may be able to recognize when they are thinking feverishly about negative things. Their expression may look stressed, disgusted, worried or scared.

You can gently ask your child what is bothering them. They may blurt it out before they have a chance to hesitate and guard their answer, which they might normally do because they are afraid or embarrassed to say it. Your child's answer may be about something minor that has put them in a state of distress, such as not being able to find something that they desperately need in that moment, like their phone or a tissue. Your child's answer may be that they cannot figure out how to reply to a text or email that they know they must reply to. It may be that your child needs to go to the washroom but they also need to get another pair of socks and put them on to keep their feet warm and they are paralyzed trying to figure out which task to do first.

As you begin to understand the types of things that cause your child such severe distress, you will realize that they truly are suffering in ways you didn't appreciate. A severely depressed person does not respond to normal day-to-day situations the way most people respond to similar situations. It is as if the simplest tasks that are required to live in this world are just too difficult.

It is through your observations and conversations with your child that you will begin to truly glimpse the magnitude of their severe depression. This awareness will help you to understand that the disorder is a mental and emotional state and not a matter of your child being lazy or spoiled. You will become more empathetic, loving and supportive as you truly realize the struggle that your child is living with.

CHAPTER 7

LET YOUR CHILD KNOW THAT THEY CAN SAY ANYTHING TO YOU

I know of teenagers and young adults who chose to end their life. So many adults around them were surprised. People said, "They had everything going for them" and "They seemed fine." I heard statements such as, "They never said anything to me" and "There weren't any signs that they were depressed."

Chances are, the teen did not express their true feelings because they did not think anyone would understand or they did not feel safe to speak to you or anyone else. Of course, there are cases where a child ends their life due to a specific life circumstance as opposed to a result of severe depression. Many cases, however, are caused by severe depression, which may not have been known to the child's family.

A teen or young adult may be able to function in society and still have severe depression. This would be cognitive depression, which can be present even when the person appears to be fine. They may be able to attend school, hold a job or participate in a sport.

If a person has vegetative depression, you are probably aware that they are depressed but you may not realize how bad it is or what the person is thinking about.

What you may not realize:

- Your child's pain is real and feels terrible.
- Your child's pain is not something they can just get over.
- Your child needs to see you actually express sympathy for their pain.
- Your child needs to hear you say "I love you."
- Your child needs to see that you know and care about their priorities, which may be very few. Their priority may be how their blanket is situated on the bed or where the phone cord needs to be.
- Your child needs to see that you are willing to listen when they speak about their interests, even if it is a topic or opinion that you don't approve of or agree with.
- Your child needs you to support their choice in a romantic partner, even if you don't approve of that partner.
- Your child may be afraid that you will die and they will be all alone.

Your child can be experiencing severe depression even though they have moments when they want to talk or interact with you. Your child may want to talk about things that don't interest you or you may have more important things on your mind. Your child may want to show you a funny or weird video on their phone and you would rather think about your shopping list, your work, other family members, or the many things you need to do that day.

It is very important that you take the time to show an interest in your child's interests. Your child may have a bit of energy at random times and want to discuss the latest show they watched or story they read or talk about the latest social media buzz. You need to sit and listen and be present with them during this opportunity. You will need to quell your own desire to try to get your child to do something productive with their current bit of energy. You may need to quiet your own mind that is thinking of all the things that you wish they could or should be doing.

Pay Attention to Your Reactions to Your Child's Interests

From an energetic or emotional point of view, you may feel a need to pull away from what your child is showing you or wanting to discuss. The topic may be something you don't agree with or maybe you and your child are on different wavelengths about the topic.

Your child may be showing you something that they want you to buy for them and you are automatically concerned about the cost and other bills that you have. Your child may want to tell you long story about social drama or a video that causes you to feel uncomfortable due to its negatively, awkwardness or for any other reason.

If the topic at hand triggers a reaction within you, try to figure out why it makes you uncomfortable. If you can identify and release your discomfort, that will be a benefit to both of you. Ask yourself, "Why did that video bother me?" or "What is it triggering in me?" This may take effort on your part and it will be worth it if it helps you to release a subconscious bias or trauma. You can also try to be open minded and see the topic in a new light or from your child's viewpoint rather than your own. You may actually learn something.

Resolving your discomfort will change the interaction with your child and improve this time together so that it can be a positive experience for both of you. See this time together as a precious gift. It doesn't matter what the subject matter is about. You don't need to be interested in or approve of the topic at hand. You can just appreciate and honor these moments with your child. It will build trust and love between you. Remember that this is time that your child is choosing to spend with you and they are not being consumed with negative thoughts in that moment.

Making the effort to pause your automatic thoughts and to fully focus on what your child is sharing with you will make a big difference in them feeling seen and heard. They will feel that their input is important to you. And it should be important to you. It is an opportunity to get to know your child better.

Validate Your Child's Interests

Your child may be checking in with you to see if their opinion of something is correct or normal. They are particularly sensitive to negative feedback at this time so it is important for you to give some sort of positive feedback even if you don't agree with their viewpoint of something.

Your child's interests will be an indication of where their thoughts and emotions are. If your child is watching funny videos, it may be an indication that they are trying to distract themselves from their pain and are trying to find something more uplifting to spend their time on. You child has the strength in that moment to make an effort to feel better.

If your child is watching crime dramas or reading about bad people, they may be using that to explore the mental condition that a person has to be in to do those bad things. It may make your child feel better about themselves because they can feel reassured that they are not doing such bad things and that must mean that they are not a bad person.

If your child is exploring the internet and inquisitive about topics, this is an improvement over them having no interests. You should respond in an intrigued manner rather than judging the content as being not worth pursuing. It may also give you a chance to see what your child is following so that you can steer them away from things that may be too negative or potentially harmful.

Remember, your child is seeking your input and approval when they share something with you. It is best to agree with some aspect of their assessment of the information. If you have the complete opposite response to a video than they do, your child may perceive that as a failure on their part. By showing you the video, they may be testing the situation to find out if their response is correct or not. Your child may be trying to get confirmation that they are a competent person and not a failure in life. Your reaction to your child's opinion of a video or event can have a significant impact on their state of mind.

If you have a different opinion to a video or event that your child is sharing with you, you could explain why you have the opinion that you have. You could clearly explain that your opinion is due to your life experience and does not mean that their impression of the video is wrong. Your child sees things very differently than you do due to their life experience. This discussion can educate you both to see things from each other's perspective. You may need to explain to your child that you can each have a different opinion about something and that it is OK to agree to disagree.

The objective is to have your child engage with you and with life. You don't have to understand their topic of conversation or even like the subject matter. If your child is reaching out to share something with you, you need to pay attention. These interactions are valuable time spent together. It gives your child some temporary relief from their severe depression and builds trust and closeness in your relationship.

Engage in Whatever Your Child is Spending Their Time On

Depressed youths are often isolated and believe that they cannot talk about what is going on in their minds or their lives. They often turn to online platforms for a distraction, for entertainment or to engage with others. Of course, there can be dangers in this but there are also many support systems that your child may have found. If you have trust with one another, your child may tell you about these contacts. This allows you to learn about and have input to your child's choices. If you do not have that trust with your child, they may turn to online connections because they cannot talk to you, and that has more likelihood of leading to bad situations.

Having an online support system may be beneficial to your child because it gets their mind engaged in something that is not self-criticism. It may reassure them to know that other youths are struggling with similar conditions. Hearing stories about how other youths cope with mental illness may encourage your child to have ideas for their own future. Their online activity may be their only activity, which is usually better than having no interaction at all.

If your child feels a need to reach out to someone to discuss something it would be good if they reach out to you. When this happens, you will need to demonstrate that you can listen to them without judgement as a parent. Listen instead as an interested person who is curious to learn and be willing to discuss random topics with an open mind.

How to participate when your child shares a topic with you:

- Make yourself listen.
- Show an interest.
- Be truly interested in learning something new.
- Don't start thinking about the other things that you need to do.
- Be fully present.
- Ask a few easy questions.
- Don't talk about depressing world events unless your child brings them up.
- Be open to seeing the topic from your child's point of view which may be something you never would have considered.
- Acknowledge that your child has an intelligent, creative or analytical mind that you can learn from.
- Be prepared to hear about new things.
- Be prepared to learn new lingo and what young people are thinking.
- Start to look forward to these interactions because you may learn something new or get a new perspective on something.
- Look forward to getting to know your child better.

Listen to What Your Child is Telling You, Even if You Think it is Strange

Your child may have found a chat group for specific interests. It may be about personal identity, relationships, world events, the environment, religion, politics, body image, skills, art, gender or sex. There are a lot of topics out there that you probably have never heard of. Ask your child to explain it to you.

Your child might be investigating a topic for any number of reasons. Listen with an open mind, as if you are a scientist rather than a parent. You should try to find a way to suspend your judgement and worry. In most cases your child is just learning about something new and finding it interesting. If your child is at home and depressed all the time, they are probably not engaging in personal relationships or their education. This exploration provides an outlet for their intellect and feelings.

Even if You Think the Topic is Unrealistic

Your child may dream of becoming a YouTube influencer or some high achievement. Even though your child cannot get out of bed or doesn't know how to set up a camera, microphone and lighting with their computer, they may need this dream of a successful future to stop the self-critical and negative thoughts in their mind. It is a good sign if your child is able to dream and be inspired by their future. This dreaming does more good than harm because it shows that your child has the ability to see a future for themselves. If your child is not thinking about the impracticality of the dream or the learning curve they would have to go through, that is OK. If your child sees the dream as a possibility, it means they have some self-confidence and some desire to live. You should refrain from pointing out the many steps that it will take or the years of study that would be required for your child to accomplish their dream. Just enjoy the dream and inspiration with your child at this time.

Even if the Endeavor is Expensive

Your child may spend hours looking at shopping sites online. The brief interest in finding something cool and buying it can be a reprieve from your child's negative thought patterns. It may also give them something to live for, when they have to wait for the item to come in the mail.

This may be difficult on you because of the expense. You need to try not to crush their one interest that is keeping your child engaged with life by saying no. Of course, you should not ignore your own fiscal responsibility and budget. You might be able to find a way to make the window shopping part of your child's enjoyment. You can try to pace out the purchasing for budgetary reasons and encourage your child to enjoy the wait and surprise when the items arrive. You could try to find less expensive versions of the item and try to turn the search into an interesting activity that you can do together. Maybe your child will become more interested in something else instead of the first item they picked out. This experience may demonstrate to your child the benefit of researching many items to determine which ones they really want rather than purchasing on impulse for the brief satisfaction it brings.

Be Willing to Learn About the Appeal of Computer Games and Online Gamers

There are many reasons why your child may play computer games or watch gamers on YouTube or other platforms. It can be entertaining to them. It can be soothing. It can be distracting. Watching a gamer is easier than trying to play the game themselves. Your child may get to know the gamers' personalities and care about their lives. Your child may consider them a friend. You should ask about your child's online friends occasionally. Encourage your child to tell you who they are following, if they have stopped following someone, and if they are following someone new.

My child told me about an amazing young gamer who died tragically of cancer. At one point the gamer joked about possibly having to get his arm amputated. Worse than that, the gamer was actually scheduled to have his arm amputated and when the doctor deviated from this plan, the doctor forgot to change the surgery schedule. The gamer and his family went in to the hospital expecting to undergo the amputation, only to find out it wasn't going to happen after all. This was an emotional roller coaster ride, and in the end, the gamer died of cancer. It was a tragic and bizarre story that any parent would be upset about. My child saw it as sad but it didn't unduly upset her. In her mind, it was just another example of the normal struggle of life. Our children see life struggles differently than we do.

Understand and Respect the Semi-Colon Tattoo

The semi-colon tattoo has a meaning in today's culture. A semi-colon in a sentence means that you could have ended the sentence but you chose not to. A semi-colon tattoo means that you could have ended your life but you chose not to. It is a sign of courage. It means that a person dealt with depression, addiction, or mental health issues that caused them to want to end their life. The person may have attempted to end their life or just wanted their life to end. The person's life continued instead. The person continued living for some reason or another and now they are glad that they are still living.

A person gets a semi-colon tattoo to honor that struggle and time in their life. It is a sign of solidarity and support between people who have gone through that experience. That time in their life was significant enough for them to want to mark it on their body and share it with others. It can also be a sign of hope. It shows that a person can get through the darkest time of their life. Your child is probably well aware of the meaning behind the semi-colon tattoo.

Seek Treatment for Your Child's Physical Ailments

Your child may experience a variety of physical ailments from their severe depression. I have learned from other families, doctors, dentists and pharmacists is that it is not uncommon for a depressed person to get infections, dandruff, hair loss, skin rashes, muscle aches, and other similar conditions. You can show support to your child by talking about their ailments and getting them appointments with the appropriate doctor.

Your child may feel better knowing that there is a treatment for the ailment, even if they realize it may reoccur if their severe depression continues. Your child will appreciate having someone acknowledge their ailment and help them treat it. This is much more effective and supportive than you trying to get your child out of bed, into the shower, or to the gym as a way to cure their ailment. These attempts just make your child feel worse about themselves because if they could do any of those things, they would have done it already. Your child is currently unable to accomplish these feats. They just need some relief from their current ailment.

Learn the New Online Words That are Used to Avoid Censorship

There are different online words and acronyms for various types of traumas that are related to mental health. Some of these have been around for a while and new ones are always getting created. The word "suicide" or "kill" is often referred to as "un-alive." The acronym "SA" refers to sexual assault. The use of these words and acronyms is partly because these words can be flagged or censored by various websites and platforms.

These alternative words and acronyms are also used to minimize the potential triggering impact they may have on a person who is watching the video. When a person uses these words and acronyms, they are showing compassion and respect to others who may have gone through a difficult time. It is helpful to get to know the lingo that young people are using or hearing on the internet, particularly when they are related to mental health.

CHAPTER 8

SELF-HARM

Society often tells us that when a person harms themselves they must hate themselves and not want to live. Yet at the same time, society also tells us that self-harm is a cry out for help or that the person just wants attention. I have learned that there is much more to the reasons why a person would self-harm.

When a child or teen's mind is on a loop of negative thoughts and worries that continues without pause for hours and hours on end, it can become unbearable. The child may do anything to find a way to make the racing negative thoughts stop. Pain accomplishes this. Pain can make the mind focus. The mind will stop its continual negative thinking and focus on the pain instead. This gives relief to the child because now their mind is quiet. Their mind is having just one thought: the pain.

If the self-harm involves blood, the child can let their eyes focus on the blood and think about the color, the feel and the movement. This focus of their gaze, their mind and their emotions can become fascinating and calming. The child is no longer thinking about what a failure they are, the many things they cannot do, or how they are a burden to their family.

This focus and calmness will be temporary and afterwards there may be an endorphin rush. The child will actually feel better emotionally as well as mentally. This entire experience may only last a few minutes or hours, but it is worth it to the child because it has paused their ongoing and repetitive negative thoughts. It may be the only way the child can actually create a better feeling for themselves.

The goal from the depressed person's perspective is to figure out a way to have the self-harm be effective on a consistent basis. This means that the injury should be minor so that it heals quickly and so that it can be caused again. It can take practice for the child to learn how to cause the injury with the right degree of pain and also be fast healing. Building up a tolerance to pain or getting an addiction to the emotional high can change this balance.

If the injury is more severe, the endorphin rush is not as effective. Ongoing and more enduring pain becomes an issue with a serious injury as well as having a longer and more painful healing process. This will cause more harm to the child's mental and emotional state because it adds intense pain to their already terrible thoughts and depression. It may cause them to hate themselves for doing it in the first place or for failing to do it to the correct degree.

Self-harm can also be undertaken as a form of self-punishment. Your child or teen may think that they are such a failure in life that they should punish themselves. In this case, they are less concerned with achieving an endorphin rush. This type of self-punishment might be in the form of taking risks and endangering their life.

Self-harm can be in the form of a new injury or by worsening an existing injury. A youth may continue to re-injure the same area over and over so that it cannot heal. This can be done to an injury that they originally caused themselves or to an injury that occurred naturally or through risky behavior. Some injuries that are caused by self-harm are more noticeable than others. You can learn to be observant and notice these types of injuries.

Types of self-harm:

- Cutting (either superficial or deep).
- Not letting a wound heal.
- Pulling out hair.
- Bumping themselves.
- Banging their head.
- Picking their nails or fingers.
- Hitting themselves.
- Taking drugs or alcohol.
- Taking risks with dangerous behavior.

Reasons why your child might self-harm:

- Self-punishment.
- To feel something.
- Focuses or quiets the mind.
- Endorphin rush.
- The pain can be preferred over their negative thought patterns or depressed numbness.
- It can be fascinating to look at.
- It allows the child to feel an emotion other than depression.

If you are quietly watchful and observant of your child's behavior, you may be able to discern if they are harming themselves. You may see that they have a homemade bandage which may be partially sticking out of their clothing. Or you may observe bruises that don't make sense if your child has not been leaving the house. You may notice that your child regularly goes behind closed doors for a length of time and is particularly quiet during those times. You may see them emerge from behind closed doors in a calmer state of mind or be able to enjoy something when previously they could not.

If you become aware of an injury, stay calm and ask your child if you can look at it to make sure the wound is clean. Tell your child that you need to determine whether or not they need to see a doctor or get stitches. Don't ask questions about how it happened, when it happened, or why it happened. Just speak calmly, as if it is just a regular injury that everyone gets at some point and it just needs a trip to the doctor or pharmacy for bandages and minor pain medication.

Depending on when you discover the injury and when you are having this conversation, your child's mind may be consumed with fear of being caught or fear that you will be mad at them and take away their tools of self-harm. Your child may be experiencing a high level of endorphins or alternatively, they may be experiencing high anxiety or adrenaline. They may not even notice the illogic of you being so calm or that you are not asking how, when or why it happened.

After you assess the seriousness of the injury and have dealt with it, you can start a conversation with your child about helping them clean things up. The child may have been so focused on the event that they may not remember if they cleaned up the mess or put away the razor blade or tool that they used. A razor blade from an eyeliner pencil sharpener or a utility knife is a common tool. You could ask where they put the blade or tool so that you can make sure it is cleaned properly. You could calmly ask them to show you where the bloody tissue is so that you throw it out. Remind your child that sterilization is important and they don't want germs to get on the tool or their injury because it would be painful and require more care if it gets infected.

Later, after the urgency has passed, you might be able to have a conversation about self-harm by asking your child to tell you how it alleviates their depression. Your understanding and acknowledgment that it has a psychological and emotional benefit, as opposed to being a suicide attempt, will make for a more constructive conversation. You may also be able to discern whether their self-harm was for self-punishment and that can lead to a discussion about why they think they should be punished. You could then reassure them that they do not deserve to be punished, regardless of whatever they may have done.

As you get through all of this, you may then be able to discuss with your child the need to find another way for them to get relief. You could explain that self-harm has the potential to become dangerous and may be ineffective or addictive over time as their body gets used to the endorphin rush. You might be able to explain to them that long term self-harm could lead to more severe injuries and potential for infection, both of which are very unpleasant and not what your child would want to endure.

Asking your child to show you the tool they used for self-harm is important. Discuss with them that it would be better to remove the temptation by limiting their access to such tools. You can tell your child that the next time they want to self-harm, to come to you instead. Tell your child that you will sit with them and talk through those difficult moments until the urge passes. You can discuss with them other options that may give them similar relief without being so harmful.

How to recognize self-harm:

- Your child may wear long sleeve shirts and long pants even in warm weather.
- Your child may tug at their sleeve cuffs.
- Your child may have bruises.
- Your child may have gauze or band-aids showing.
- There may be blood drops on tissue in the trash.
- There may be scabs or cuts or scratches that don't seem to heal.
- There may be injuries or wounds that don't heal as fast as they should.

How to react:

- Do not freak out.
- Stay calm and ask to see the injury so that you can determine if it needs medical attention.
- Do not ask how, when or why it happened.
- Calmly ask your child if you need to clean up the room where it happened.
- Say that you should go check the room just to make sure everything is cleaned up.
- When you get to the room, ask your child where they put the blade or tool. If they ask why you want to know where the tool is, tell them that it is because it is important to determine if the tool is clean.
- Ask where your child put the tissue or towel so that you can see how much bleeding was involved.

What to do after the urgency has passed:

- Tell your child that you understand that sometimes self-harm can be soothing.
- Ask your child to tell you how it feels to them when they do it.
- Tell your child that you love them and want to help them find a safer way to cope.
- Suggest that there may be other ways to calm the mind.
- Tell your child that you will help research to find a better solution for them.
- Tell your child that you love them and you are here for them.
- Suggest that the next time they want to harm themselves, to come to you instead.
- Say that when they come to you, you will do whatever they prefer (i.e. talk or not talk) and that there will be no judgement.
- Encourage your child to help you think of new ways to stop their mind loop of negative thoughts.
- Talk about videos they have watched, food that they like, maybe have a cold refreshing beverage.
- Tell your child something positive about themselves.

The main thing for you to understand is that a depressed youth often sees self-harm as a positive. It is a coping mechanism. Although it can also be self-punishment which is negative treatment towards themselves, neither type of self-harm is your child attempting to end their life.

Your child will likely be afraid to show you or talk to you about their self-harm because of all the types of judgement and ramifications. It may be too multi-layered for your child to explain it to you. Once you demonstrate to your child that you know they are self-harming, you know that it can be helpful at times, and you just want to help them deal with the injury, their fear of getting in trouble may pass. This should ease some of their stress and open them up to discussing it with you.

Even if you have managed to talk about your child's self-harm and feel like you both have a grasp of it, you need to be aware that the endorphin rush can become an addiction. Your child may or may not even realize that they are addicted to it. Their severe depression has them so low that they may not be able to stop their desperate need to feel better.

Getting your child off of this addiction is important and will require steady monitoring, especially during the very low points. The earlier you catch the self-harm the easier it will likely be to break the habit. You will have to be more engaged than ever in talking to your child and being around and available to help them get through these particularly tough times when they want to turn to the one thing that they know will make them feel better.

Your child may turn to other habits that could become additions like drugs or drinking. Alcohol and some drugs like marijuana are depressants and not likely going to be used by your child as an endorphin rush. Depressants are more likely going to be used by your child to numb their mind or as self punishment. Other drugs and dangerous or risky behavior can be stimulants and create the endorphin rush or be used for self-punishment.

Your child may not be able to attend support groups so you may need to find in-home professional support. There are also some coping methods that they can try that are similar to their self-harm but safer.

Other coping methods your child could try:

- Wear an elastic on their wrist and snap it.
- Write on their body with an ink pen.
- Write positive affirmations on their body.
- Do something that will give a sharp sensation such as biting a lemon or ginger root.
- Squeeze ice or put an icepack on part of their body.
- Flatten cans for recycling.
- Hit a punching bag.

As you have conversations with your child about self-harm and their evolving experience with it, you may find that it is not an addiction. Your child may be in control of their choices and not likely to do it impulsively.

You may also discover that your child learned their method of self-harm from a peer. This may cause you to want to speak to the peer or their family. You should discuss this with your child first, who probably has some insight into the peer's situation. You do not want to intervene without knowing the circumstances. This may be something that you should discuss with your doctor or therapist before getting involved, so that the proper steps can be taken.

Most doctors and therapists will ask young people who are struggling with mental illness about self-harm. The doctor or therapist will probably ask your child in a private session, when you are not present. In all likelihood, the doctor will not discuss self-harm with both you and your child in the same session unless your child says that they are comfortable doing so.

CHAPTER 9

CONSIDER ALL THE TREATMENT OPTIONS

Society says that the best way to treat severe depression is with both counselling and medication. Both of these take time, money and effort. Counselling is usually in the form of a social worker or a psychologist. Medication is usually by way of a family doctor or psychiatrist. All of these may involve undergoing tests, blood work and assessments.

Sometimes the professionals will come to your home but usually you have to go to their office, depending on where you live and the options available to you. The level of success can be dependent upon how well your child fits with the practitioner. Does your child like the person? Is your child comfortable confiding in the person? If, after a reasonable effort, it is not a good fit, then it is worth trying to find someone else. When you switch doctors, your child may be required to undergo another assessment that may involve lengthy questions and answers. Your child may not be up to undergoing yet another assessment when you switch doctors. It can become a balancing act between deciding whether to switch doctors or to stay with the ones you have.

There are also alternative treatments available in different countries. You may find yourself needing to explore these options. I am not trained or equipped to discuss the details about any of these treatment options. I will just share with you a bit about our experience and some of what I have learned from other families and various medical professionals about different treatments.

Psychological Counselling

My child spoke to more than 30 doctors and counsellors over a seven-year period. She is currently seeing two doctors. My child has been told that she has learned all of the standard tools and mental exercises available for the treatment of depression, anxiety and OCD. These usually start with Cognitive Behavioral Therapy (CBT) as a general tool and "logical thinking" for anxiety. We were told that the only real treatment for OCD is "exposure therapy" which is particularly unpleasant.

None of these tools are easy and they all take time and effort before you will know if they are effective. My child got so skilled at understanding and carrying out the exercises that the doctors and counsellors told her that there was nothing more they could teach her. The doctors and therapists could be there for moral support but that was all they could do at that point. Sometimes, even just moral support from a professional is worth the effort of getting out of the house to see them. It will probably help your child to know that there is a counsellor or doctor who believes their struggle is real and is willing to try to help.

Medication

There are so many medications. The medications can be mixed and matched based on the combination of mental health disorders that your child has. It is very important to know for sure which disorders your child is suffering from before trying out medications. This is because if your child is given something for a disorder that they do not have, the medication may cause significant side effects and potentially cause harm.

Random people are quick to suggest that your child has ADHD or is bi-polar when that person knows very little about the actual condition or your child's true symptoms and are not trained in this medical field. There are many various medical assessments that can be done on your child, varying between mildly tedious to burdensome. Your child needs to be properly assessed and diagnosed. Your child will likely find some relief in knowing which disorders they have and which disorders they don't have.

We were told by doctors that sometimes you just have to keep trying one medication after another until you find one or a combination of more than one that works. The problem with this is that you have to wean your child on and off of the medications. The weaning period can take weeks or months to know whether a new medication or combination of medication works. Your child will likely be worse off during this transition period. It can sometimes be a terrible and dangerous time. Depending on your situation, it may be better to stay on a medication that barely works than to risk changing to another one. Sometimes the side effects are so bad that your child is worse off in a whole new way. You may have to add yet another medication to counteract the side effects.

Trying New or Alternative Medical Treatments

There are new and alternative treatments that are being used by the medical communities in different countries around the world. They may already be in your country or you may have to travel elsewhere to get access to them. You can research treatments and you should discuss them thoroughly with your doctors. Some may be risky and many will likely be unpleasant. They may or may not work for your child.

Depending on the age and maturity level of your child, you should review alternative treatment options with them and let them have input on the decision. Your child's willingness to undergo a treatment will depend on their current level of severe depression and their comfort level with the treatment. Some of these alternatives will require multiple treatments. This means getting your child out of the house on a regular basis for an unpleasant or risky treatment that may or may not work. It is important that your child be willing to undergo the treatment before you commit to it.

Treatments recognized by the medical community in various countries:

- CBT (cognitive behavioral therapy)
- Medication
- rTMS (repetitive Transcranial Magnetic Stimulation)
- Ketamine
- Psilocybin and psilocin
- Electroconvulsive (shock) therapy
- Sleep deprivation therapy

Alternative Treatments That are Recognized by the Intuitive Healing and Psychic Community

Many children are very intuitive and have extrasensory abilities. They easily feel other people's moods and thoughts. These children may tap into the mass consciousness without even realizing it. If you can discuss these things with your child to help them understand it, it can be reassuring for them. If your child can learn to recognize the difference between their actual feelings and thoughts and the feelings or thoughts that they are picking up from others, they can learn to avoid and discard what they are sensing from others.

If you have intuitive or energetic healing skills, you could work with your child by using these tools to help ease their emotional pain. If you do not understand any of this, you can still help. You could find a psychic, channeler, reader or energy healer to see your child. It should be someone who is open to your child asking questions. There are many readers and channelers in communities and online that you could look into.

What can be helpful to a child with severe depression is learning to discern the difference between their feelings and the feelings that are coming from another source. It could be a memory that they are picking up on, it could be past trauma inside their own energy body, it could be a situation that they are feeling telepathically. With all the current wars and world-wide awareness and discussion of negative events, these children can pick up on the negative energy and feel the suffering of others quite easily. It can seem very real to your child and cause them distress to feel the negativity as well as having the view that they cannot do anything to help the people who are suffering.

If your child learns to recognize and use their perceptive abilities, they may be able to direct them into positive pursuits rather than absorbing so much fear and negativity. Your child may be able to develop their intuitive and extrasensory skills so that they could be helpful to other people. Your child may be able to find a like-minded group that seeks to spread positivity. This may give your child a goal to pursue and they may start to feel better about themselves by helping others.

Some energetic and intuitive healing techniques that may be helpful:

- Qigong (Chi healing)
- Shamanism journeying and soul retrieval
- Taoist dissolving meditation
- Past life regression
- Intuitive energy healing
- Channeling
- Internal martial arts (using chi)
- Yoga (using prana)
- Breath work
- Visualization
- Reiki
- Mediumship
- Psychic readings
- Various forms of meditation
- Tapping
- Acupressure and acupuncture
- Massage therapy
- Sound therapy
- Chanting

Take a Break Sometimes

Even with your child applying many tools and techniques, they still may be severely depressed and not be able to function in society or take care of themselves. If your child falls into this category, there may be a time when you need to allow them to take a break from trying so hard to get better so much of the time. It is OK for them to take a break from the constant effort and endless treatments. I'm not saying that they should go off their medication. I'm saying that sometimes it is OK for your child to relax and stop applying the techniques and tools for a while.

The constant trying to get better and doing the work can put a mental and emotional strain on your severely depressed child. Taking a break may allow your child to rest and just focus on living, even if they primarily stay in bed. It gives them a chance to take a break from the devastation that dashed hope can bring. Let your child be depressed and be in bed with no expectations. This may actually give them some relief from the constant trying to get better and failing to do so. It may give their mind a break from telling themselves that they are a failure and can't accomplish anything.

Most health care providers do not want to encourage their patient to take a break from therapy or let go of hope because it is perceived as giving up. It also goes against the healer's objective of helping their patient by trying to find a successful treatment or cure. There is a fear in society that if the severely depressed person gives up on the hope of getting better, they may choose to end their life.

What I have learned is that the severely depressed person has most likely already thought about ending their life. Having one's hopes dashed over and over again can be very detrimental.

Sometimes having a new acceptance of never getting better can actually give them a break of trying to "fix" themselves, and this acceptance could lead to a less stressed condition.

Sometimes, for a period of time, you just have to let your child live in their severe depression without you both always trying to make it better. This may give your child some relief and will show them what their life could be like if they have to live with their severe depression. This temporary rest may allow new insights to come to them and may lead to an improved emotional state which could renew their hope for getting better.

Another benefit to taking a break is that it will relax the energetic vibration associated with pushing against something, such as an illness. The law of attraction tells us that all that effort and focus on fighting something can actually keep that thing present in one's reality. Sometimes, by accepting a situation (such as an illness) and seeing it as a temporary condition, is a better mindset for allowing solutions to come through.

Discuss Long Term Care

If your child has lost all hope of getting better, or is about to lose hope, it may be time to discuss how their life might be if they have to live with severe depression long term. Your child may need to think about and accept living their life this way. You can discuss who and what will be their support system as the years go by. You can discuss finances and who in the family or circle of support might be willing to take over once you are no longer able to be their primary carer. You can also look into home care services in your area.

Having this conversation about your child's long-term care can make it real for them. It may be upsetting to your child but it can also be reassuring once they know that there is a plan in place. It becomes a different thought process when your child can truly admit and accept that this is their life for the foreseeable future. The comfort of having a long-term plan may improve their outlook, which previously may have been to scrape through each day, just hoping for it to end. This thought process may also jolt your child's mind out of its repetitive negative thought loop and remove their fear of you dying and being left all alone.

Choosing Treatments

As parents and carers to a severely depressed child, you may ask yourself if you should treat it with conventional methods or seek alternative treatments? I think the answer is to do both. You should research and discuss with appropriate professionals the various treatment options, the potential side effects, the chances of success, and the long-term maintenance requirements. Depending on your child's age and maturity, you should include them in making these important decisions about their treatment and care.

CHAPTER 10

HAVE THE TALK ABOUT MEDICALLY ASSISTED SUICIDE

"I want to die!"
"I want to go home!"
"I don't want to be here!"

Your child may be wailing these words in despair. Or your child may be whispering these statements to themselves. Either way, it will probably crush your heart. My eyes teared up as I heard my child suffering. I could feel my body clench as I tried to tolerate the terrible situation.

Severely depressed children and teens often go to sleep wishing that they would die in their sleep. Some severely depressed youth have these thoughts every night for years. They are so disappointed and sometimes devastated when they wake up and realize they are still alive and have to endure yet another day of misery. Your child at this point probably would have tried over and over again to get better, yet everything has failed and they feel completely trapped and hopeless.

Have you asked yourself if you want to be there when your

child ends their life? Have you thought about whether you would rather hear about your child's death from a police officer or if you would rather find your child after their suicide? When you realize that these might be your options, you may finally have to ask yourself if a person has a right to choose whether to live with severe depression or not. If there is no solution and all of the efforts have failed, is a person trapped or obligated to live their life this way? Would you want to live your life this way? How long should a parent or society force a person to live a terrible life with no end in sight? The legal answer is different in different countries. The moral answer is based on your personal belief system.

At some point, you may need to mention the fact that some countries allow medically assisted suicide. If you don't bring this subject up, your child probably will. You need to be open to discussing this topic with your child. Of course, this option is only available if your child is a legal adult. There are usually several long steps that have to be followed in order for a person to be eligible for medically assisted suicide for mental illness. You could tell your child that you are willing to research the rules for your country and other countries. If your adult child has already done the research, this tells you that they are serious about ending their suffering and they want to know their options.

The age of your child is an important consideration when framing this conversation. Even young children may want to discuss the options of life and death. A teen should be able to understand the laws, age requirements and conditions around medically assisted suicide. If they are a legal adult, they may qualify for medically assisted suicide.

The knowledge that there may be a medical way to end their life will likely make your child feel better. It may ease their mind and give them some comfort. Instead of pushing against their constant pain and fearing that it will never end, they may feel hopeful that there is a way out and that they don't have to live this way forever. Having this information may make it easier for your child to tolerate their current state and any remaining time that they may be alive.

Knowing that they may actually have a choice and the freedom to choose will give your child some relief. Having this discussion with your child will be worth the relief that it brings them. This conversation may change your child's entire perspective because now they know there is a safe way out and that they are not alone in exploring the options.

Your teen or adult child will likely have some sense of what a massive sacrifice it is on your part to even have the conversation with them. Your child may not say it out loud, but they probably greatly appreciate your support and willingness to take part in this discussion. Intellectually they know you love them and that this option goes against your parental instincts. For you to have this conversation with them demonstrates your love on a whole new level.

One of the things that people don't talk about is that a child with severe depression feels terribly alone and frightened. This is on top of their feelings of being unworthy, unloved and a failure. They feel guilty and trapped. When you have the discussion of medically assisted suicide with your child it shows them that they are not alone and that you truly understand that their pain and struggle is real.

The knowledge that there may be a medical way out and that your child does not have to face the effort and planning of ending their life on their own, can be empowering for them. If your child knows that you will be there with them when they end their life, it can make them feel loved and supported. Your child will not feel so trapped. It will likely take the edge off of their desperation and despair. It may also alleviate some of the guilt they feel at the idea of leaving you to cope with their suicide. This relief may also cause them to have new hope and give them energy to keep living.

Yes, the Discussion Will be Hard for You

I heard the well-known saying in my head, "If you love someone let them go." I never imagined that I would be applying that phrase to this scenario. In addition to the grief I felt when I thought about it, I also felt very hurt. I felt hurt that my child would choose to leave me. But of course, this situation is not about me. It is about my child who is very, very sick and suffering terribly. I thought about the roles and responsibilities that parents and children have to one another.

Should parents always be there to support their child regardless of their age and condition? Does the child have any obligation to be there and support the parents? Different cultures would answer these questions differently.

I realize that having the discussion of medically assisted suicide with your child is a difficult concept for you to entertain. Society tells us that if we talk about it, it would be the same as endorsing the idea. However, there is a good chance that your child has already thought about it. You avoiding the subject does not mean that your child will not research the option on their own. You can make it very clear to your child that you would prefer that they not choose medically assisted suicide, while at the same time explore the possibility with them.

You cannot prevent this option by avoiding the discussion. If your adult child is set on ending their life, you can actually help them by discussing this monitored way of doing it. It is possible that having this conversation will result in your child not choosing to commit suicide. Your adult child will be comforted to know that they could choose to end their life with medical support and with you by their side. Your child probably realizes that for you to go to this extreme to support them, is because you truly understand that they are in severe pain and you love them enough to be there when they choose to end their life.

You will find that most countries have a very clear process to evaluate potential patients and it requires a psychological evaluation by more than one doctor over a specified length of time. If you would need to travel to another country, this will lead to a discussion about saving money for the trip, which can also take time. A thorough evaluation of this option will give your child something to think about and plan for, which means they will be committed to live during this evaluative period. During this evaluative period, the relief your child feels may bring new hope that improves their condition, which could lead to their ultimate choice to stay alive.

Other, Related Conversations to Have Before Dying

Once you both start taking about the possible choice for your child to medically end their life, it will likely lead to other conversations. You could discuss what things your child may want to do before they die. Your child may not have ever given this any thought. Thinking about what they may want to do before they die may lead to your child finding reasons to live. These reasons may include both short-term and long-term goals.

Your child may ask you what you plan to do with your life after they are gone. Their ability to ask about you and consider your feelings and future lifestyle may be something that they hadn't seriously thought about before. Your child may not want to impose pain on you or put this burden on you if there is another option. Your child might also need reassurance that you will find a way to get through your grief and move on with your life.

After discussing these topics with your child, they may become open to discuss nearly anything with you, particularly if they know that you won't overreact. Once your child knows that you accept that they may die sooner rather than later, they may tell you the different ways that they have thought about ending their life. Be prepared. This can be jarring if you haven't given it any thought.

You will need to think about the possibility that your child may not be here long term and you may watch them die. By accepting this, you can mourn the thought and then move forward with your child by creating a bucket list of what they want to do before they die. You can share those experiences with your child and create memories.

Things your child may want to do before they die:

- Get a tattoo or piercing or both or many.
- Travel to a particular destination.
- Buy a specific item.
- Do a special activity.
- Play and succeed at a particular computer game.
- Try a specific food dish.
- Have a relationship.
- Go to a special show or concert.

Think about how you will live your life
if your child dies, such as:

- Will you continue working?
- Is there an opportunity to improve relationships with other family members?
- Do you have interests that you would pursue?
- Would you offer your support to others?
- How will you memorialize your child?
- How could you turn the situation into something meaningful?
- How will you avoid becoming depressed?
- Will you give yourself time to grieve?
- How will you grieve?
- How will you move on?

Having the discussion about what your child might like to do before they die may focus their mind and raise their emotional state. You can investigate together how to accomplish the things on their bucket list. It may become an enjoyable time for the both of you and help lift your spirits.

I imagine that parents whose children have a terminal illness wonder how they will ever be able to go on after their child dies. This is probably one of the hardest things to endure as a parent. The knowledge that your child will die before you and potentially when they are young, must cause immeasurable pain.

When you child has severe depression, thinking or knowing that your child will die is not usually part of a parent's thought process. We spend our time thinking and hoping that the severe depression will eventually lift and our child will get better. Or we think that they will be living with severe depression indefinitely. It is a bit of a leap for our minds to accept that our child may actually die from their severe depression. And another huge leap to think about assisting our child with their death.

This is precious time together, especially once you realize that your time with your child may be limited. Your acknowledgement that your child's life may be short term, may lead you to appreciate every moment that you have with them in a whole new way. After you have gotten past the sorrow and acceptance that their assisted suicide is a real option, having this new-found appreciation and love for your time together can be beneficial.

Your child may choose not to end their life after all. What is very important to understand is that having these conversations means that your child is less likely to end their life impulsively on their own. The chances of you coming home to find that they did it without you, is less likely to occur. You may not have a police officer knocking on your door informing you that your child is gone forever.

CHAPTER 11

WHEN YOUR CHILD IS GETTING BETTER

It may be the medication. It may be the counselling. It may be the chi. It may be the universe. Who knows why your child got better. It was probably a combination of things. Your child's recovery may be a very slow improvement or your child may suddenly show a distinct improvement.

Sometimes the medication can create a jittery energy and your child will start pacing around the house looking for something to do with their restless energy, yet the mental motivation is still not there. This is frustrating for your child because the medication gives them energy but their mind still lacks interest in things and their emotions may still be sad or listless.

This recovery period is a time to appreciate your child's improvement and you will need to adjust to a new reality. You still need to be fully supportive to your child without being too encouraging or expectant.

You could try to direct your child's attention towards a subject that used to interest them before they were severely depressed. Don't suggest that they start doing chores or taking a shower. If your child is actually walking around the house, you need to understand that this, in and of itself, is an improvement. Maybe all they do is pace and be jittery. Even if they are irritable, it is better than being depressed in bed or thinking self-abusive thoughts.

Don't push your child to go outside or to listen to music or to call a friend. They aren't ready yet. Your child is just getting used to moving again. Their body may have muscle aches or energy blockages as they adjust to being mobile again. What you can do at this point is observe your child as they move around the house. Your child will likely start talking to you more as they are becoming mobile again.

Pursuit of Living and Having Multiple Interests

Once your child starts to venture out into the world, they may want to make up for lost time and have several things they want to pursue. They may want to buy a lot of things or buy online courses. Your child may be impulsive and they may have forgotten how to moderate their choices. They may be frantically interested in something and then once they get it or order it they move on to something else. Your child may forget why they wanted that thing so badly after they become interested in something else.

You will have an adjustment also. Of course, you will be very relieved to see the improvement in your child. You may find yourself juggling much more than you had to before. It may be overwhelming at times. You may have trouble keeping up with your own work and responsibilities while you try to respond to your child's renewed energy, which may be flying in many different directions at once.

This recovery period can be a bit of a balancing act. It is

important to encourage your child's endeavors to a reasonable extent because your child is still very susceptible to self-doubt and self-criticism. When you disagree with their interests or endeavors they may perceive your difference of opinion as yet another failure on their part. They need reassurance that they are thinking correctly and are not wrong or completely off base about something. You may need to explain that the two of you can have a difference of opinion and it does not necessarily mean that either one of you is wrong or right.

Financial Cost of the New Normal

Many of your child's new-found interests will cost money. This will likely be another adjustment for you. It is important to be supportive of your child's interests and not complain about the cost too much in front of them. Instead of telling your child about the cost or saying that you cannot afford it, try to discuss with your child the number of activities that they are pursuing. You can discuss how the activities are all worthy and interesting, but it would be best to prioritize them and maybe undertake them a few at a time. You could gently mention how you should budget to afford them as opposed to just saying the item is too expensive or not worth the expenditure.

I recommend that you try to choose things that can be refunded and make peace with the things that cannot. You will be better off if you can make peace with the financial expense. It may help to consider the expenditure as a cost of your child's recovery or a form of therapy. Just try to keep it manageable so that you don't exhaust your financial or emotional resources. To be clear, I am not saying you should go as far as considering this "retail therapy" in the casual way people use that term. I am just pointing out that when your child is in recovery there are naturally going to be financial costs as they start to live their life again.

You also need to try not to complain to your child about how you spent money on an endeavor that they then gave up. If you start disregarding their interests or saying "no" to their desires because they have neglected a previous purchase, your child may perceive this as you no longer being a safe and supportive parent. Your child is probably well aware of their change in direction and that it cost money. They are probably harboring guilt about that. You don't need to point it out. You could try to encourage a brief waiting period, during which your child can think about the activity to make sure that the interest is going to endure before making the purchase.

You could ask your child to tell you more about their current interest and explain to you why they would like to pursue it. You should show a willingness to learn about the topic, even if you don't particularly like the topic at hand. This will allow your child to engage their mind in something they are interested in before the money is spent. This mental engagement with new pursuits will help establish a more positive thought pattern and emotional state. These new patterns should eventually replace your child's previous self-abusive thoughts and negative emotions. It may also strengthen your relationship with your child. As a bonus, you may learn about many new things.

You may find that suggesting a less expensive alternative may have a detrimental effect on your child's mindset and emotional state. This is why you need to speak positively about what they chose rather than always suggesting something different. There is a lot of your child's self-worth wrapped up in their selection and whether you approve of it or not.

You should review your child's pursuits to make sure they are healthy and reasonable. You could ask your child to send you the websites so that you can review them to help prioritize and keep up with all the things they want to pursue. It may also be worth explaining to your child the amount of time it will take to fully enjoy or participate in each chosen endeavor. Your child may like or want ten different things but only have time to pursue three. This may be something that your child has not thought about.

In some ways, you will need to teach your child these reasoning skills because they may not have learned them if they have been severely depressed in bed for years. Even if your child is an older teen or young adult, if they have spent years as low-functioning or non-functioning they may not have learned these skills. Your child may need guidance in this and other areas of life. In some aspects, your child may be behind in mental and emotional development and in other ways they may be more mature than their years.

Do Encourage and Don't Direct

Do listen and participate when you child explains to you their latest interest. Don't try to direct your child to finish school, participate in family activities, or fulfill responsibilities instead of pursing their new-found interest. This will not work. It may crush your child's new motivation and they may tell themselves that it is not worth trying to get interested in anything. The idea of school may be a mountain of regret, shame, and guilt that your child just can't face at this transitional time.

Some people may think that this approach of tiptoeing around your child's feelings is coddling or too much effort on your part. When you see your child start to get better it is easy to want to just treat them like you would anyone else. If they show an improvement in one area it is easy to assume they are better in all areas. You will have a strong desire for them to be completely better and you may make the mistake of treating them as if they are fully healed.

I remind you that your priority at this time is to keep your child alive. Your child is still in a dangerous place, even when they are showing improvement. You also do not want to damage the good relationship of trust that you have built up with your child by suddenly being less compassionate or impatient with their recovery.

This is a very critical time because your child's mind is just venturing out into positive directions. It is very important to your child that you validate their attempts at re-entering the world. You don't want to do anything that would shut it down.

See Your Child's Changing Interests as an Exchange and Movement of Energy

If your child gets interested in many things, makes plans for those things, and then loses interest, try not to let this frustrate you. Especially if you have spent money on those things. From an energetic point of view, the pursuit of interests is your child reaching out to the world. They are moving their energy and that involves putting energy out and allowing energy in. Your child needs to engage with the world by reaching for something. You want them to engage and be interested in the world. This phase may be lifesaving for them.

Physical things and intellectual learning are forms of the exchange of energy. Life is an exchange of energy. It costs money usually because of how our society is structured. The flow of money is a flow of energy that is always moving in and out, coming and going. Try to allow the flow of energy to come back to you in the form of your child's health and try to appreciate other benefits flowing to you as you adjust your work schedule around this new reality. Your child's ability to gain knowledge will lead them to becoming more well-rounded, which will serve them in their life ahead.

This financial and energetic investment in your child's new-found interests is truly easing your child back into the world. When the item was purchased, it improved their mind and emotional state. They were showing an interest in life. The various interests engaged their mind and emotions which is much better than when their mind and emotions were crippled with depressive thoughts. The money may be gone but it was not necessarily wasted.

Sometimes your child pursues one thing after another as a way to keep their mind engaged so that they don't slip back into their depressive thoughts. Your child may also feel a desperate need to pursue various endeavors as a way to make up for the lost time when they were not functioning. Your child's active pursuit of multiple interests may also be their way of chasing a good feeling. They have been feeling bad for so long that when something makes them feel better they may be desperate to repeat the action that caused that good feeling. It may take some time for your child to have the confidence that they can slow down their pursuits and it will not bring back their depression.

At this time, your child is showing an interest in life for the first time in a long time. As they continue to get healthier your child will learn to get better at managing their multitude of interests and their changing priorities. Their mind will begin to prioritize and focus on the more important things rather than being spread out in so many different directions.

How to adjust your lifestyle:

- Get over the shock of your child being engaged with life.
- Embrace having so many more things to juggle.
- You may go from having not much to do or schedule for your child to having too much.
- Be prepared and available to catch your child if they fall.
- Don't assume a setback is going to send them all the way back into severe depression.
- Have a back-up plan for every endeavor.
- Gently explain that it is OK if they give up on something and that it is not a failure.
- Your child may try to make up for lost time and may need help prioritizing.
- Be cautiously optimistic but don't assume everything is going to be normal from now on.
- Lean into the unfamiliar.
- Always find something positive to say when your child talks about a subject.
- Do not criticize anything your child does or wants because that may trigger their bad feelings about themselves.

Your New Relationship with Your Child

You had developed a way to cope when your child was severely depressed in bed or when they were barely functioning on auto-pilot. You worried about them while you tried to carry on with your own life. Now you may have to drive them to events or places and review purchases that they are pursuing. You may now worry about how their event goes and whether something will happen to trigger a bad reaction. All of this can be overwhelming at first as you adjust to the new normal.

Your child may be a legal adult by this point. You may have to re-establish your relationship parameters because your child will likely want to have some autonomy. Some discussions will still be in your roles as parent and child due to their lack of development during their time of depression. Other discussions will be appropriate as the roles of two adults.

You may have to explain this new relationship to your child and work together to establish new communication styles. When you both begin to view your child as a young adult rather than a sick child, they will likely rise into that role and show even more improvement.

Your child may start to be interested in your life and other family matters. You should follow their lead on this and not inform them of too much information too soon. You don't want them to be burdened with family issues or responsibilities until they are able to handle it.

CHAPTER 12

BAD DAYS AND FEAR OF RELAPSE

During your child's recovery, there will probably be some setbacks. There may be times when functioning in society becomes too much or too tiring and your child will weep or yell and crawl into bed. When this happens, just tell your child that it is OK and help them get comfortable. Let them vent to you or fall asleep. You don't have to solve their problems right then, just be a supportive listener and get them what they need.

When your child gets overwhelmed with living in the world, their mind may struggle with the desire to just go to sleep and never wake up. This most likely is their need to have a break from society and from living life, and not necessarily a serious desire to leave the world.

You and your child may have a fear that they will relapse into severe depression. There may be times when your child is terrified that they will sink back into severe depression if they did not manage to brush their teeth or if they fail to do another activity that they had been managing to do recently. This can cause them emotional and mental anguish. You should remind

YOUR CHILD WITH DEPRESSION

them of their accomplishments and reassure them that a bad day does not mean their severe depression will return.

Paralyzed with Indecision

If your child is having a moment when they are overcome with the inability to make a choice about what to do next, you may need to help them break through their paralyzing distress. This can occur when they are having a very difficult time trying to force themselves to accomplish something that they had been able to accomplish recently. Your child may feel that if they don't accomplish a particular task, it is a personal failure that may lead to their former state of severe depression. If your child is a high achiever, they will be particularly hard on themselves if they cannot do something that they feel that they should be able to do or that they had been able to do recently. This inability to make a decision will likely cause your child's anxiety level to rise which can trigger an intense fear. It is hard for anyone to make decisions when they are operating from a place of fear.

You could help your child through their distress by telling them that it is OK for them not accomplish a particular task in that moment. The dilemma may be whether to fall asleep without brushing their teeth or to stay home rather than to attend a particular event. You may need to talk your child through the pros and cons of their options regarding the dilemma. It is important to explain to your child that any choice is valid and does not mean that they are a failure if they choose to not push through an activity. You may also need to explain that if they choose to not do something that they feel is important, it does not mean they are bad or slipping back into severe depression.

You could help by discussing with your child how they might feel if they do the activity versus if they do not do the activity. Your child will most likely say they would feel equally bad about either option. It would be helpful for your child if they can learn how to determine which choice would cause them the least amount of mental and emotional distress. It is important to encourage your child to learn to use this exercise in a positive light by thinking about which decision feels better rather than which decision feels worse.

You may have to walk your child through the steps of each option. If your child is tired and overwhelmed, their anxiety or other conditions are more likely to be heightened and triggered by the various steps of each option. If you have an understanding about how their mental health conditions interact with one another, it can be helpful.

One example of this dilemma may be your child feeling overcome with fatigue and extremely stressed about the need to brush their teeth before bed. They may be in a state of physical pain and mental anguish over this decision. You could talk them through the choice of not brushing their teeth and going straight to bed compared to the choice of struggling through the steps to brush their teeth and then going to bed. You can help your child figure out if they would feel better going to bed right away even if they have some regret about not brushing their teeth or will they feel better once they get in bed feeling proud that they brushed their teeth even though the effort was an upsetting struggle that made them feel even more exhausted?

Another example might be your child agonizing over going to an event. You could ask your child how they will feel if they were at the event. Would they feel afraid and anxious or would they feel proud that they accomplished the task of attending? You can also ask how they would feel if they stay home. The idea of staying home probably makes your child feel safer, but it may also make them feel guilty or consider themselves a failure.

It is important to help your child understand that either choice they make is fine and that the goal is to make a choice so that the pain of being paralyzed with indecision can end. You may need to gently remind them that by not making a choice, that can sometimes become a decision by default.

For example, if your child's paralysis about deciding whether to attend an event extends past the start time of the event, that will cause your child to miss the event. This may be something your child did not consider and the added time pressure can worsen their distress. But if you do not point out this fact, they may be equally upset once they realize the event start time has passed and they no longer have the option or time to decide. Either way, it is likely very hard for you to watch them struggle with this seemingly simple decision.

If you feel any sense of amazement that the situation is causing such a huge internal battle for your child, you will get a sense of just how powerful a mental disorder can be. You may be inclined to speak loudly or harshly to your child to snap them out of their trapped state of mind. You should be aware that when your child is operating from this high level of fear that any harsh word from you will be particularly frightening to them. Try to moderate your voice and words so that you speak calmly and firmly rather than harshly.

Once your child makes their decision about the current dilemma, you should remind them that making the choice was an accomplishment and that they should feel good about having done that. It is also important to encourage your child to feel good about the choice that they made and to let go of any guilt or regret they may have about it.

This technique will serve your child in their future by teaching them how to think through various options and anticipate associated consequences. This exercise won't always be focused on how a particular decision will make them feel because they will learn to expand their thought process to include how a decision may impact others. Your child will have learned how to make thoughtful decisions and to stand behind their choices with confidence.

Bad Days that Cause Your Child to Give Up on an Important Pursuit

If something bad or discouraging happens in your child's day or over an extended period of time, they may have the reaction to quit an important goal that they had been pursuing. The bad experience may cause them to view the entire subject matter through a negative lens. Your child may want to give up on the entire endeavor or may suddenly lose all interest in something that they previously loved.

For example, your child may no longer care about the end goal of earning an educational achievement and the doors that it could open for them. This situation may be devastating to you because you watched your child enjoy something and actually be happy about something and now they have no interest in it and want to give it up. It is hard to understand how they could change their view of something so completely.

When you see your child happy about something, you likely have a strong desire for them to stay on that path. Not to mention the financial and time commitment that you both may have invested into the subject matter. You could try to gently remind your child that the subject matter still has merit and it was something that they used to enjoy and were good at.

You may have to accept your child giving it up at this time. You can keep the door open for your child to return to the subject at a later date. Don't discard the items, such as text books or supplies. Just set them aside and within reach for when your child is interested in that subject again. It is possible that your child will come back and revisit the subject at some point in the future. If, over time, your child does not renew their interest in that subject matter, you could sell or donate the items to a good cause.

Manners and Social Cues

Your child may have developed some bad manners from being depressed for so many years. They may be blunt with their words or have a communication style that other people may not fully understand. You too, may have developed a short-hand style of communicating with your child. You may have to work on your own communication style to assist with your child's interaction with the outside world.

Your child may have unusual mannerisms if you have constantly helped them over a long period of time. Some parents have always opened the door and pushed elevator buttons for their child. I knew one mother who always handed her child whatever item they needed before the child even knew they needed it. You may have to start holding back from this type of overprotection and teach your child to fend for themselves.

Gently pointing out your child's bad manners can be tricky and it may depend on their tolerance level for receiving your suggestions. Your child may react badly to what they perceive as your criticism. You may have some hesitation about providing constructive criticism because you are concerned that such a discussion will cause your child to regress from their recent improvement. You can soften the conversation by pointing out some positive aspects of your child's accomplishments and then move into one constructive suggestion.

You might be able to carefully teach your child some appropriate social cues. Other socially acceptable behavior, however, might be more impactful if your child learns on their own or from others. There will be some situations that your child will understand very well and other situations that they do not. Your child may be offended if you explain something that they already know or be angry if you have not explained something.

You may need to wait until your child asks you why a person reacted a particular way to something they said or did. When you explain that maybe your child did not express themselves clearly or politely, they may get confused and upset about it because they perceive this as yet another failure on their part. You may need to reassure them that it is not a personal failure because miscommunications and awkward interactions happen to everyone. Remind your child that they did not intentionally cause the miscommunication and that maybe the other person was just having an off day.

Your child may perceive someone else's comments or actions toward them as more negative than they were intended. When your child explains a situation to you, you should bear in mind that the situation is coming from your child's worried perspective. They may be interpreting the situation more severely than it actually was. This does not negate the seriousness or minimize the impact that the interaction has had on your child, but it may mean that the other person is not as concerned about it. You could remind your child that every person is coming from their own point of view and that maybe there will be an opportunity to address the matter with that person the next time they are together. You child may want to avoid that person indefinitely or act as if nothing had happened. As time passes and your child's mood improves, the situation may not bother them as much.

Your child may be nervous about making phone calls or video calls. Similarly, your child may or may not be comfortable navigating computer applications such as arranging for a ride or ordering food. This is relatively common with people who have general anxiety and it could also be due to your child not having socialized for years during their severe depression. This social skill, like others, can be learned from practice and your child will get better at it as they get more experience with it.

You could walk your child through the exercise by explaining various scenarios of what the other person may say when they answer the phone and what your child can say in response. You could set up a practice video call so that your child can become familiar with the process. These practice sessions will allow your child to be calmer when the actual call or video has to be made and they will learn to practice scenarios on their own when they are nervous about something.

Larger and More Adventurous Pursuits

Your child may want to travel or take a course in a city far away. They may want to live on their own. In your child's mind they may be desperate to accomplish a significant goal. They want and need to prove to themselves that they are better. They may have a strong need to prove that they can actually live life without your help and they likely have a desire to make up for lost time.

Your child's adventurous ideas will probably worry you. You should be supportive and start discussing the minute details of what their life will be like when they are living alone and without your support. How and where will they buy groceries?

What meals will they make for themselves? How and when will they do laundry? How will they comfort themselves on a bad day? How often will they clean their apartment? You could set up a communication plan with your child to speak to each other every day or several times a day while they are away. You should discuss with your child a back-up plan and be available to fly out and bring them home if necessary.

Adjusting and Accommodating Your Child's Tired Days

Your child may have tired days that look similar to their depressed days. Your child may exhibit the same signs of hating life or be numb and unresponsive. You will be relieved when you see your child get up and out of bed after having a bad night. As this occurs over time you will begin to realize that your child is capable of joining life again more easily, which is different than when they were severely depressed. Maybe that bad day was just your child being tired or overwhelmed.

Your child's brain is learning to process and function after a long period of being on a negative loop. This can take time. It may be months of your child learning and adjusting to living life again. Particularly if your child was severely depressed for years.

The healing takes time to seep into each aspect of your child's life. They will eventually learn to cope with disappointment, with being overwhelmed, having fatigue, and managing large and small disappointments. You will see these capabilities improve.

Your child is also having to live with the awareness that their mind may be playing tricks on them. Your child has to learn how to recognize when their thoughts may not be an accurate representation of what is taking place. Learning to cope with the awareness that they cannot always trust their thoughts and reactions to something can be upsetting and difficult.

Slowly but surely your child should be able to manage their thoughts and feelings and maintain an interest in living their life. The human spirit is strong and you will see it begin to stir after being inactive for so long.

Once your child's brain chemistry and energetic vibration really starts to change, the positive moments should prevail and eventually outweigh the negative. Energetically, once your child has a higher vibration, some incredible positive experiences may manifest. It may be a bit bumpy at first with good things happening in random small areas of their life. Some things will work out and some will strangely fall through, only to reveal a better thing coming next. If you both learn to observe these patterns, it will be easier to see a setback as an event that is actually making room for something better. This could become a fun and hopeful way to live life.

Even though your child may fall apart from time to time, they are better than they were. You can remind them of their accomplishments and tell them that they do not have to make up for the time they lost when they were severely depressed. Your child can start from where they are on any given day and take it one step at a time. Remind your child that it is OK for them not to be perfect and they do not have to do everything right all of the time. Tell your child that their current state of health is a wonderful improvement over their previous severe depression and that it is just fine to venture out into the world at a slow and steady pace.

As your child continues to get better, eventually you both will have the confidence that they really are going to stay better and that they will be able to handle the ups and downs of daily life.

CHAPTER 13

DISINTEREST IN THEIR LIFE

After your child has been better for a while they may go through a period where they are not interested in their life or disappointed with how it is turning out. Even though your child has had several accomplishments since they were severely depressed, they may view their life as a series of failed dreams or wasted efforts. They may be bored with life or overwhelmed with how difficult it is to succeed.

Your child may look back at all their various pursuits as failures because they had lost interest in them or the pursuit did not work out. Alternatively, even if your child's pursuit did work out, they may have changed direction and discarded their achievement.

This dissatisfaction your child is experiencing is not the same as when they didn't want to live at all. This is more of a lack of interest with how their life is turning out. Your child may be going through a phase of not being able to find anything that interests or motivates them. They may be seeing what their life has become, which they view as being not very accomplished.

Maybe your child had high hopes when things were getting

better. Your child felt that they could finally get on with their life and fulfill their dreams and destiny. If your child now perceives life as just mundane living and sees the world as being below their high standards, they may come to realize that they might have to settle for something less than what they want or believe they should be able to achieve. This can be a heavy blow to your child's heart and mind.

You would think that your child's renewed vigor and energy would give them an enthusiasm for life because they can finally live again. The times when the new medication suddenly gave your child energy and they were zipping around the house expressing interest in various things made it seem like they were looking forward to living their life. It may be surprising for you to see your child lose interest in their life. This dissatisfaction with life may come early or later in your child's recovery.

Even though your child is awake and has re-engaged with life, they may not know how to start putting their life back together. Their brain cells are not used to being consistently interested, motivated or enthused. It may take some time to get past this phase.

Your child may not remember that they felt happy when they got their new job. They may not be able to remember the good feeling they had when they accomplished something. It is fascinating and alarming to be talking to your child when they say they do not remember specific achievements or joyful moments that you shared. Your child may retreat into the familiar sadness and want to give up on participating in life.

During this phase, you could remind your child that this is just a temporary pause and they just have to take it one step at a time. You could encourage your child to be kind to themselves and allow themselves to relax and take a break from their multiple pursuits. Your child is still not used to telling themselves positive affirmations or thinking kind thoughts about themselves.

You will need to persevere through these low times and remind your child of their talents and positive aspects. Have a look at the Abraham-Hicks Emotional Scale to see that disappointment and boredom are more than halfway up the scale. Reassure yourself and your child that things will get better and that this low time is just a few steps away from contentment and optimism.

New Questions About Self Preservation

If your child is deeply dissatisfied and not caring to put effort into their life, you may wonder if it will lead your child to make poor choices because they don't care enough about their life to protect themselves. The poor choices in this case are less about self-punishment and more about just not caring what happens to them. Your child may not have the motivation to put in the mental effort to think of something better or find of a way out of a bad situation.

It may help your child to talk through their dissatisfaction and you could remind them to remember that things are better than they were and to not give up hope that their situation will get even better. You may want to encourage your child to stay close to home and away from potential pitfalls during this time.

You may ask yourself if there is something, anything, that will get your child interested in living their life? Will they always be dissatisfied? Is there something inside of your child that really doesn't want to be here? If this phase persists, you both may wonder if it will carry on for the rest of their life. Is living with dissatisfaction enough? Can your child live in a state of disappointment or boredom?

Even with your child's recent improvements, their brain chemistry may not be where it needs to be. You may need to discuss their current medication with their doctor and consider a change. It is good to discuss the pros and cons of changing a medication with your child and review the side effects that they may have experienced in the past. Your child may not remember these details from their previous medications.

This phase should pass as your child's brain chemistry, emotions, and energy continue to improve. Eventually your child will likely show a renewed interest in life which will prevail over their disinterest and dissatisfaction. You child should be able to maintain their interests for a longer period of time and sustain the positive emotions that the new interest brings. This renewed outlook should get more substantial and viable over time and lead them to have a more satisfying life.

High Achievers

Many young people with anxiety and depression are high achievers. This causes them to put extra pressure on themselves to succeed and to be extremely hard on themselves when they don't measure up to their own high standards. What other people might just shrug off, your child may dwell on, agonize over and see as a failure. Being a high achiever causes additional distress because they almost always believe that they should have done better.

Your child probably focuses more on what they haven't accomplished rather than what they have accomplished. They may feel that there is still a mountain to climb before they are a full and independent adult. If they were severely depressed for years they are probably very upset at having lost those years and now they feel behind in their life. This can make them view their future as requiring many long years just to catch up with their peers.

Sometimes, the things that bother high achievers the most, is when people criticize them. Especially when the criticism is based on false assumptions. If your recovering child is mistreated or misunderstood, or if they cannot realize their dreams and goals, they may ask, "What is the point?" Their extreme effort to re-engage in society only to be treated badly is very upsetting to them. It may take some time for them to process this disappointment and get to a place where they can sustain their confidence despite other people's judgement.

My child has always had high standards and a strong moral compass. She couldn't understand why people would settle for anything less than what was fair, right and honorable. Sometimes high achievers cannot comprehend how people can be so negative towards others. This feeling is similar to what we all feel when we see injustice and suffering in the world, but it seems to be so much more pronounced in many of the young people today. Seeing the younger generation hold to their high standards has helped me raise my own standards.

How to Get Your Child Interested in Life Again

Most people have felt dissatisfied with life from time to time. How do we get out of it? Under normal circumstances we may read self-help books or pursue something that interests us or find a purpose. These suggestions will not work with someone who is severely depressed. These methods might be effective with someone who is in the recovering phase from severe depression.

You could suggest to your child that they pursue a cause that would help make the world a better place. Many of them care deeply about the world's future. Your child may like this idea or it may be too much effort at this time. Your child's reaction to this suggestion will depend on their state of mind when you have the discussion. They may need time to sit with their disinterest and just focus on doing their daily routine. Even that is a big improvement from where they used to be.

Your child's disinterest in life may be an issue of having some residual repetitive thoughts about wanting to leave the world. You could check in on how they feel about long-term care or medically assisted suicide. In all likelihood, they are no longer interested in those options. The discussion may help your child to re-assert their desire to live, which should help change their residual negative thought patterns.

Now that your child has re-entered the land of the living, and has found it to be unsatisfactory, where do you go from here? How does one break through the dissatisfaction with life? Enthusiasm is usually the most impactful solution. But how does one get enthused about something if a person is thoroughly dissatisfied or indifferent with what life has to offer?

Topics that may renew your child's interest or generate enthusiasm with life:

- Remind your child of their accomplishments.
- Talk about their talents and positive traits.
- Show admiration for their ability to cope with specific difficult circumstances.
- Ask your child how they feel about a recent or past interest. See if the discussion will lead to a new interest.
- Find a way to laugh and lift the mood.
- Work together to dream big to find something your child can get excited about.

- Suggest doing something easy and enjoyable (i.e. go out for a treat).
- Mention bigger dreams that they have talked about before (i.e. travel).
- Tell your child it is OK to have several interests that are now sitting idle.
- Reassure your child that they can come back to the pursuit later, when they are ready.
- Revisit your child's bucket list of things they want to do before they die.
- Remind them that this phase will pass.
- Let your child sleep to give their mind and mood a break.
- Let your child take a break from their constant efforts to accomplish something.

You could walk your child through their achievements in a way that shows how far they have come. Try to do this in a way that does not compare or dwell on past difficulties. Instead, you should speak of it in a way that demonstrates that small and large goals are within reach and show that you believe your child is capable of achieving them. Remind your child of their dreams and how satisfied they will feel when they reach those milestones.

After a sleep, your child may feel better. The positive thought patterns and brain endorphins that they have accumulated should eventually prevail over the disinterest. Your child should get better at reminding themselves of the good things in life. They may be able to notice that they are capable of handling difficult situations. Your child should become more able to keep their larger goals in mind, which may motivate them to endure the daily difficulties. Ultimately, your child wants to feel better.

Try to find a way to laugh with your child. Laughter lifts one's mood. Laugh about a current joyful moment or about anything random. When your child was in deep depression, laughter is usually too far away. Now though, you should be able to access laughter even from their current state of dissatisfaction. Watching a comedy may help lighten their mood and open the way to more positive thoughts.

It is important to remember that your child is living in the world again. They may be experiencing occasional mild depression rather than severe depression during this time. You could re-visit some of the tools and methods that helped in the past. Your child's emotional state will change from time to time and from topic to topic and will likely improve when they pick up on a new interest. Re-visit the emotional scale to remind yourself of where your child is on various thoughts or subjects and review the nearby steps that lead to a higher vibration.

Your child may spend the rest of their life struggling with varying degrees of depression. They may need to make plans for their life to have ups and downs. Their life endeavors may have starts and stops. You can help by showing your child how to adjust or delay their short and long-term plans. You can remind your child that it is not their fault if they get depressed and cannot carry out a plan or a goal. Help your child find a way to cope with living a life that gets interrupted with depression.

CHAPTER 14

MY STORY

My daughter had both types of severe depression over a nine-year period. She also has anxiety and OCD (obsessive compulsive disorder). She still suffers from occasional bouts of depression and overwhelming feelings of sadness that seem to come out of nowhere. This entire experience has made us question the purpose of our lives, ponder the meaning of the human experience, and gave us a better understanding and appreciation for the quality of life.

We saw more than 30 medical professionals in a decade. We had group and individual therapy. She had personal assessments from several specialists. She was diagnosed several times by different doctors. She tried many different medications and combinations of medications. She underwent repetitive transcranial magnetic stimulation and tried sleep deprivation therapy. We considered Ketamine and electroconvulsive (shock) therapy. She had readings by spiritual teachers and healers. We did qigong, shamanic healing and dissolving Tao meditation.

I had to get past the guilt, the questioning, the blame, the sorrow, and the worry to a place where I could accept that this was our life experience. Instead of always trying to figure out how to solve it, I had to allow her to have the experience. I needed to stand by her side and make it as comfortable for her as I could. I had to accept that it was my experience as well.

This experience broke down so many of my belief systems as each of my attempts to alleviate her severe depression failed. I had to learn that my role was not to solve her severe depression but instead to experience being her support system and to learn from it.

The situation made me re-evaluate my life. I had to accept that on some level I must have chosen this life to be here to support her. I sensed that we were a team and that we agreed to be here together. I wish I understood all of the reasons why this was our life experience. During that time, I had to accept the reality that my most important goal of each day was to get her through the day. It was one day at a time. Sometimes it was a critical few hours at a time.

At times, the amount of abuse my child imposed on herself mentally and emotionally was intense. Her mind was her own abuser. How could I protect her from her mind? That was when she had cognitive depression. At other times, she was overcome with vegetative depression. Her mental and emotional state would consist of an overwhelming sadness and a deep, smothering feeling of not being able to move or function. It is truly astounding to see how the human body can shut down for days at a time.

Sometimes all I could do was be her support system and keep myself as healthy as possible so that I could assure her that I would not die and leave her. We went through phases of trying to fix it, phases of discussing whether to live with it or not, and phases of acceptance. All phases were exhausting.

Some important things that my child has taught me:

- Do not joke about mental illness.
- Do not be ashamed of mental illness.
- Respect that mental illness is a real disorder.
- Having mental illness does not mean you are weak.
- Realize that a person will likely question whether life is worth living with their condition.
- A person cannot snap out of it.
- A person cannot "think positive" to get out of it.
- A person cannot "find a purpose" to end it.
- A person cannot go outside or get sunshine to cure it.
- Other people shouldn't need to understand it in order to accept that it is real.

My child had various body aches and pains during her severe depression. She lost muscle mass and I believe that she stopped growing. She had been an athlete as a child and young teen. She had been lean and strong. During the severe depression she looked frail and weak. She often had no interest or life in her eyes.

One doctor said that "Some people are treatment resistant." Another doctor said that he was not optimistic about her recovery. He told me that he expected that this would be a difficult case and he prepared himself for the long haul when she became his patient. My daughter remembers watching one doctor after another lose hope. She remembers seeing the hope drain from their eyes as her sessions with them went on and on without improvement. She felt guilty about being the patient that they could not help.

Remembering how my daughter had been a playful, athletic, happy, and motivated child and seeing her now as a non-responsive teen who slept most of the time was heartbreaking. I asked myself, "What happened?" and "What did I do wrong?" I wondered if it was caused by this event or that event. I agonized over whether she experienced a trauma that I was not aware of. Over time, I learned that there is no point in getting caught up in these questions. It would just bring me down and take away from my ability to be positive and supportive.

It is an amazing thing, what severe depression can do to a person. My child was alive yet barely living. She wished to die every time she went to sleep. She wanted to leave here and go back "home" where she could be happy.

Like many young people who have anxiety, my child was an overachiever. I told myself in a sad joking manner that, of course, she would be very good at having severe depression. She would be excellent at it. Maybe on some level she intended to be the best she could be at severe depression, and that it would be the most severe case the doctors had ever seen. Maybe after she believed that she had achieved an extremely high level of severe depression excellence she would allow herself to let go of that goal and move on to a different and healthier goal. Or so I hoped.

My child told me on more than one occasion that she had lost all hope. She said that every time she had hope that some new technique or medication would work, and then when it didn't work, it crushed her. She didn't want to hope anymore. She said that the crushing disappointment was too painful and devastating. It was sometimes easier for her to just succumb to the severe depression and lie in bed and wish for death. It had become too much effort for her to think a positive thought. It was often too much effort to distract herself from her negative thoughts by watching a video or trying to slip into unconsciousness.

She just wanted it to end.

For a while my daughter wanted to know what was the likelihood that she would never get better? She pushed each current doctor to tell her. One finally admitted that about 20% of severely depressed patients do not get better and have to live with it. The doctor acknowledged that she was potentially in the 20% category. My child found this information to be satisfying because it proved that she was not imagining her terrible condition. Doctors don't want to tell you this because they think it will make the patient worse. Having this information did not make it worse for my child. It validated what she already knew. She knew that she had a hopeless, severe depression that may never end.

My child did not die in her sleep or otherwise. She finally got better.

My child's improvement was a combination of things over a long period of time. We had been doing qigong and other energy treatments for years. Her new medications finally made a difference and took the edge off. Her mood was still sad most of the time but she was able to take care of herself and re-engage with the world.

I remember one particular moment when my child had a significant breakthrough. She was having an anxiety attack in the car outside of her martial arts class and we were working on removing it with our energetic healing methods. She was able to locate where the fear was manifesting in her body and we were able to dissolve it. This time, when the anxiety and fear left her body, it was really gone and did not reveal yet another layer of pain. She was like a new person and was able to get out of the car and go to class with a bounce in her step and joy on her face. It was the first time in years that I had seen her in such a positive state of mind. It was truly shocking to see her go from complete paralyzing fear to confident and composed.

After that day, things continued to slowly improve. She worked three part-time jobs for a few months. She worked 18 days in a row at one point, all by her choice. She enrolled in a local college. She enjoys baking and cooking again like she used to. She has many different interests which she pursues enthusiastically. She socializes with other people, which does not exhaust her the way it did in the past. She is able to handle setbacks and mediocre days. Her anxiety and OCD are also less severe.

Of course, some negative life experiences have happened to my daughter as well. She was bullied by three adult classmates at her local college. Her ability to endure this poor treatment for multiple weeks and still excel in her course astonished and impressed me. When the college chose to protect the three bullies rather than her, it caused a significant setback. All that strain caused her to leave the college and it took several weeks before she was able to get back to where she had been in terms of her enthusiasm and interest in life.

There have been other bumps along the way. For a while we worried about a full relapse. There hasn't been a full relapse but there have been sad days, upsetting moments and some looming depression. Thankfully, she is able to recognize it and we try to fend it off with the tools we have. We slightly adjust her mediation occasionally, which sometimes works and sometimes does not. We still see her doctors on a regular basis. Fortunately, my child is better able to tolerate and endure the low points. Sometimes we just have to wait it out.

Unfortunately, depression may always be an occasional aspect of my daughter's life. It may interrupt her pursuits from time to time. Until it doesn't. One must always keep the door open to hope that the depression may end for good.

I learned that my daughter is the strongest and bravest person that I know. She nearly always tried to do the work and use the tools that she was taught. I am able to envision my daughter with a bright future once again. When I had these visions during her severe depression, they were far away and felt like a dashed dream. Now, the visions are stronger, clearer and they feel within reach. I can see my daughter's momentum carrying her forward safely and steadily.

I have gotten to the place where I trust my child's ability to function and keep herself safe. She is capable of living on her own and knows how to get through the difficult times if she has a setback. I believe that she has the mental and emotional control and capacity to solve any problems she may encounter. My daughter knows how to get help, if and when she needs it.

What this experience has revealed to me is that my child has amazing strength and fortitude. Instead of the severe depression making her weaker than the average person, it seems to have made her stronger. My daughter and I have a close and strong relationship because of what we have gone through together. I have great respect for my child and I admire her courage, integrity, and spirit.

CONCLUSION

I wish that I had a magic solution for you. I cannot guarantee that my suggestions will prevent a bad outcome for you and your child. However, I do believe that the suggestions offered here will make it easier for you and your child to survive their severe depression. My sincere intent is that these suggestions will keep your child alive so that you both can get to a place of trust, hope, improvement and happiness.

When your child is suffering from severe depression, it is not their fault. It is not something they can get themselves out of or they would have done so already. Your child is not lazy or privileged. Your child is not weak. Your child is suffering from a smothering mental disorder and they need compassion, love and unconditional support.

Some people may suggest that all the depressed child needs is tough love to get them out of it. This, and other societal views are too simplistic and outdated. You may find that you need to discard society's expectations and avoid bad advice from people who do not understand the true nature of your child's disorder. Kindness and understanding will help your child the most, and build trust between you.

It can be very difficult to live with a person who is suffering from severe depression, particularly when it is your child. You will have a strong desire to make your child well as soon as possible. You will want to find a cause so that you can solve the problem. You will probably have to let go of this desire and many others. You will have to change your expectations for your child's life and focus on their care and maintaining your own mental and emotional health.

You may need to have difficult conversations with your child about long-term care, self-harm and assisted suicide. You may have to research alternative treatments in various countries. You will likely become less rigid in your thinking and find yourself to be more openminded and perceptive.

You cannot force your child's improvement. Sometimes, despite all your efforts, you may just have to wait it out. You may have to accept that their severe depression is here to stay, at least for the foreseeable future. If you can see your child's severe depression as an experience rather than a bad thing that you have to cure, it makes the experience a bit easier. Try to accept your role as their support system with the purpose of seeing your child through the struggle rather than fighting against it. Your goal is to keep your child alive so that they can get to the point where they can function again.

The objective at any given moment is to learn to live with the illness while still holding a vision of your child being better. Not "getting" better, but actually "being" better. There is a subtle and very important difference between these two viewpoints. If you can hold positive thoughts and visions of you both being well and happy, it may help the recovery come sooner.

Sometimes a severely depressed person cannot imagine a positive future, so you may have to hold these visions for both of you. You could imagine your future self, looking back at this time as a special time when you reached deep inside yourself to be consistently patient, loving, and supportive. Envision yourself in the future, when things are better and you are feeling thankful that your child's severe depression is in the past.

Your child's recovery may take weeks, months or years. You may have to accept that your child will become an adult before it gets better. Even when your child is functioning again, they may be burdened from time to time by depression.

It can also be quite an adjustment for you when your child begins to get better. The recovery period has some surprising challenges. You may spend time and money on several different pursuits as their new-found interest in life expands. You may learn about random subjects that you have never heard of before. You may have to teach them how to function in society.

This experience will change you. You will change from who you were before your child's severe depression was part of your life. It will change your personality, your belief systems, and your priorities. It may break you down and you will have to build yourself back up. This experience has the potential to make you a better person.

I am a better person because of my daughter in general, but also because of our experience through her years of severe depression. It has made me more patient and compassionate. Her high moral compass has made me examine my belief systems and change them for the better.

I hope that the information in this book is helpful to you so that you can help your child and yourself as you both navigate through their severe depression. You will likely discover that your child is braver and stronger than you ever imagined.

Remember to tell your child that that you love them, over and over again. Please be kind to yourself as well.

Printed in the United States
by Baker & Taylor Publisher Services